Above:
Ski-equipped Gloster Gamecock II used for fighter training at Kauhava, 1939/40
Below:
Gloster Gamecock II, LLv 24, operating with Lentoasema 1 at Utti in the early thirties.

FINNISH AIR FORCE 1918-1968

Text by Christopher F. Shores

Illustrated by Richard Ward

Compiled by Richard Ward and Christopher F. Shores

ACKNOWLEDGEMENTS

We would like to thank the many friends without whose help the production of this survey of the Finnish Air Force throughout its first fifty years would not have been possible. They are alphabetically:

J. Alexander, G. Botquin, C-J. Ehrengardt, B. Hielm, G. Kamphuis, W. B. Klepacki, K. Niska, E. Ritaranta, M. Salo, Finnish Air Force, United States Air Force.

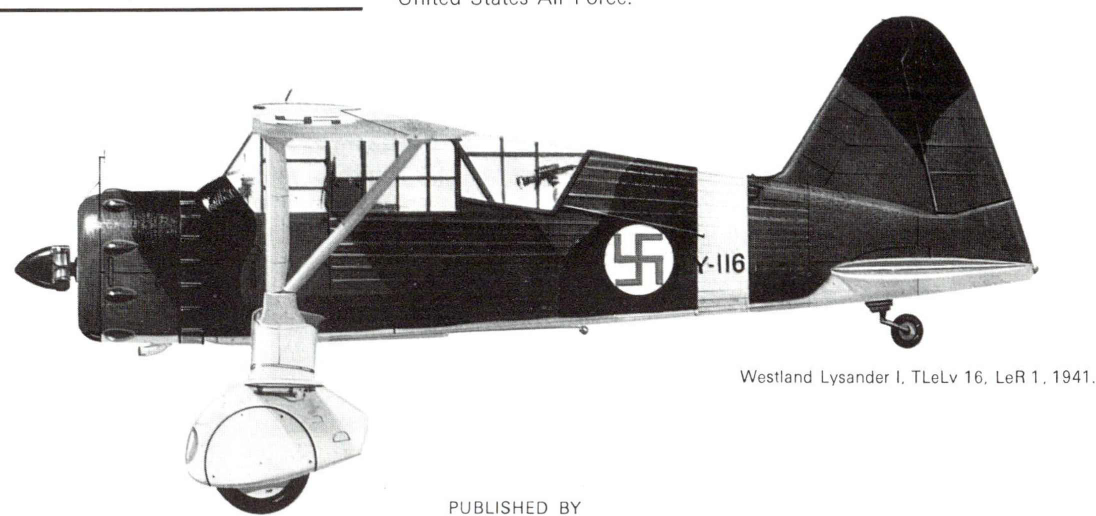

Westland Lysander I, TLeLv 16, LeR 1, 1941.

PUBLISHED BY

Arco Publishing Company, Inc., 219 Park Avenue South, New York, N.Y. 10003

First Published by Osprey Publications Ltd. and Printed in Great Britain

Library of Congress No. 75-93936 · Library Edition SBN 668-02122-5 · Paperback Edition SBN 668-02121-7

Above: MiG 23UTI conversion trainer of HavLv 31 taking off. (K. Niska).

Above: MiG 23F shows to good effect its delta planform.   (K. Niska).

Left: Beechcraft 17 of the Liason Flight at Malmi, 1956. Overall silver scheme.   (K. Niska).

Below, right: V.L.Viima II primary trainer.
(E. Ritaranta).

Above: Focke-Wulf Stieglitz primary trainer, 1957.   (K. Niska).

Below left: V.L.Pyry II.   (K. Niska).

Note: Standard trainer scheme, olive drab green fuselage and deep orange wings and tailplane, lettering in white.

Above: Fieseler Storch photographed during the fifties. The aircraft is ST–112.   (K. Niska).

Right: D.H.C.–2 Beaver of the Transport Squadron at Utti.

Left: Hunting-Percival Pembroke Mk. 53 of the Transport Squadron used for aerial photo-surveying. The aircraft is here seen at Malmi. (K. Niska).

Fokker D.XXI tactical-reconnaissance fighter of TLeLv 12 during the Continuation War.

THE FINNISH AIR FORCE, 1918–1968

Shortly after the start of the Russian Revolution in 1917, the Finns seized the opportunity to break away and form an autonomous state, their War of Independence, fought between the Finnish Red Guard and White forces under General Gustaf Mannerheim, beginning on 6 December 1917. Late in February 1918 the White Army was presented with its first aircraft, and on 6 March a second arrived, like the first, from Sweden; it was presented by Count Eric von Rosen, who flew the aircraft, a Thulin D, to Finland. The machine was marked with his own personal good luck symbol, a blue swastika, and this was adopted as the national marking to be applied to all aircraft of the new air force, the Ilmailuvoimat, 6 March 1918 being taken as the day of formation.

A Commander-in-Chief, Flying Forces, was appointed on 10 March, so that the Finnish air force was an independant arm right from the start, and as further aircraft were acquired, Flying Division 1 was formed at Kolho, near Tampere, Flying Division 2 being formed a little later at Antra, near Viipuri. A motley collection of rather elderly aircraft were gathered into these units, including Thulin Ds, Nordiska-built Albatros B IIs and C IIIs, D.F.W. C Vs, and various types captured from the Russians including Nieuport 10 and 23s, and Shchetinin M5, M9, M15, and M16 hydroplanes and flying boats, a total of 47 aircraft of 19 different types. These aircraft undertook some reconnaissance flights and a little pamphlet and bomb dropping, but made no great contribution to the situation before the war ended in May 1918 in Finland's favour. The surviving aircraft soldiered on for two or three years after the war, but were steadily replaced as the air force was put on a more adequate and permanent footing.

During the rest of the year consolidation took place, certain flying stations built by the Russians being taken over, and a little training was undertaken, a number of German specialists being invited to the country to advise on these matters. At the same time a number of recruits were sent to Germany for training. The revolution here, and the end of the First World War, caused these to return home, and assistance was sought from the French instead, a mission from this country arriving in 1919. The following year an Aviation Force Aircraft Factory (Ilmailuvoimien Lentokonetehdas) was set up, and on 14 October 1920 a Peace Treaty with Russia was at last signed.

The new Aircraft Factory negotiated a licence for the production in Finland of the Hansa-Brandenburg W 33 monoplane floatplane, known here as the I.V.L. A 22, the first of 120 examples being delivered in 1922, and in 1923 a major procurment programme was completed, the majority of types being purchased from France, these including 38 Breguet XIVA-2 reconnaissance-bomber aircraft, and 12 Georges Levy Type R flying-boats, which had arrived in 1919, and 20 Gourdou-Lesseure GL 21 fighters which arrived in 1923; 3 Caudron C.59 and 30 C.60 trainers followed 19 earlier Caudron G.IIIs, and from Britain 15 Martinsyde F.4 Buzzard fighters were purchased from the Aircraft Disposal Co. A manufacturing licence for the Caudron C.60 was also negotiated, and 34 more of these were built.

In 1923 the first fighter training course was set up under Oberleutnant E. Thuy, a German 'ace' of W.W.I., the Martinsyde Buzzards being used as advanced trainers, and in 1924 the first fighter squadron was formed under Capt. E. Könni with the GL 21s. Three Flying Divisions were now set up:—

Flg. Div. No. 1 at Utti; Fighter squadron with GL 21s, Ground Reconnaissance squadron with Breguet XIVs.

Flg. Div. No. 2 at Viipuri; Bomber squadron with Breguet XIVs.

Flg. Div. No. 3 at Sortavala; Maritime squadron with Hansa A.22s.

In addition there was a Flying Battalion at Santahamina, outside Helsinki, where the Aviation School flying mainly Caudron C.60s was based.

At this time also the air force was given the task of aerial photographic surveying of the country, a duty which it still performs to this day, and in 1924 a British delegation arrived to advise on the future planning and organisation of the force. This delegation, having regard to the very large number of lakes in Finland, recommended a concentration on seaplanes, and in consequence in 1926 the fighter and reconnaissance squadrons at Utti were combined into one unit as the sole land-based operational squadron, the bomber squadron at Viipuri converting to Hansa A.22s. British influence was to remain dominant for some years, and most officers of the air force undertook at least some part of their training in that country, until well into the thirties.

During the twenties it was the policy of the Finns to purchase samples of various aircraft types to test before placing quantity orders, and at the same time the national factory began turning out a number of prototypes of its own design, so that a large number of varied aircraft saw

The original Thulin D presented to the Finnish White Army on 6 March 1918 by Count Eric von Rosen. (E. Ritaranta).

service in ones and twos during this period, including 2 Spad S.34s, 2 L.V.G. C.VIs, a Fokker D.X, an Adaridi, an Avro 504K, a Potez 25 and 6 Morane-Saulnier MS 50s; from the factory came single examples of the I.V.L. C.24 and C.VI.25, of the K.1 Kurki, and of the D.26 Haukka I fighter (this latter was followed by 2 examples of the improved D.27 Haukka II).

Procurement continued in 1926 when 12 Koolhoven FK 31 two-seater fighters were ordered from Holland, followed the next year by one Fokker C.VD and one C.VE. Following evaluation of these, 13 more of the E model were ordered later. Meanwhile in 1927 8 Aero A.11 reconnaissance-bombers were ordered from Czecho-slovakia, and two Gloster Gamecock IIs from England, 15 more of these being built under licence in the 1929-30 period. In February 1928 the Aviation Force Aircraft fac-tory became the State Aircraft Factory (Valtion Lentakone-tehdas), and the following year turned out the first nation-ally-designed aircraft to go into production, the Sääski trainer, also producing 10 of 22 D.H. Moths which were to be built under licence, while the Czech Aero factory delivered 16 more reconnaissance-bombers, this time A-32s. Late in 1929 a licence was acquired for the production of the Blackburn Ripon IIF, convertible for land or float-plane use, and the first of 26 of these was delivered two years later.

At the end of the twenties some great changes were instituted in the training organisation of the air force, which had been re-titled Ilmavoimat, Santahamina being given up as the main pilot training centre in 1929, Kauhava in East Bothnia being developed for this purpose instead. In 1931 the first course for reserve officers was run, followed three years later by similar courses for N.C.O.s, while courses were also instituted for prospec-tive squadron commanders, a highly-trained cadre thus being formed with a large reserve to call upon.

By 1930 the air force consisted of a Detached Ground Flight Squadron at Suur-Merijoki equipped with Aero A-32s and two Detached Maritime Flight Squadrons at Tervaniem and Sortavala, a third being in the process of forming at Turkinsaari, all these flying the Hansa A.22 floatplanes, other surviving aircraft either being in store, or used for training. The State Aircraft Factory was now turning out more training types, the home-designed Viima and Tuisku, and the Czech Letov S.218A Smolik. During 1930 a Junkers W.34 transport aircraft was pur-chased from Germany, and in 1931 5 more were ordered, together with 6 of the K.43 bomber variants of the design, these aircraft being equipped to operate on floats most of the time. At the end of 1933 17 Bristol Bulldog IVAs were ordered from Great Britain, and despite some delays due to problems concerning the supply of their engines, all these fighters had been delivered by early 1935.

The air force was still mainly equipped with float-planes in the mid thirties, and there were only two land bases, but it was becoming increasingly clear that land-based aircraft would always enjoy a higher performance, and consequently a considerable re-organisation and ex-pansion programme was planned, bases being designated as semi-autonomous Flight Stations (Lentoasema), each having certain units attached, and for the first time these squadrons received numbers. Although the economic depression of the time caused considerable cut-downs in the planned expansion, after reorganisation the air force was disposed as follows:

Lentoasema 1 at Utti: LLv 10, Sääski IIs and Moths
  (awaiting operational equipment) for reconnaissance

Caudron G–III trainer, coded 1E15. See colour illustration. (E. Ritaranta).

and close support.
LLv 24, Gloster Gamecock II fighters.
Lentoasema 2 at Santahamina: LLv 36, Blackburn Ripon
IIFs and Hansa A.22s for maritime reconnaissance.
Lentoasema 3 at Sortavala: LLv 38, Blackburn Ripon
IIFs Hansa A.22s, and V.L. Kotka IIs for maritime
reconnaissance.
Lentoasema 4 at Turkinsaari: LLv 34, Blackburn Ripon
IIFs and Hansa A.22s for maritime reconnaissance.
Lentoasema 5 at Suur-Merijoki: LLv 12 , Fokker C.VEs
for reconnaissance-bombing.
LLv 26, Bristol Bulldog IVAs for fighting.
Lentoasema 6 at Viipuri: LLv 44, Junkers K.43s, bom-
ber floatplanes.
For training there was an assortment of types including
Letov Smoliks, Sääski IIs, Moths, Martinsyde Buzzards,
and Aero A.11s and A.32s.

This was to remain the basic structure and equipment
until late in the thirties, when the increasing tension in
Europe brought a crash programme of re-equipment and
modernisation, and of expansion, which was ordered in
1936. The same year in an effort to implement this, 18
Bristol Blenheim I bombers were ordered from Great
Britain, and the Fokker C.X reconnaissance-bomber was
evaluated in Holland, 4 being purchased. In 1937 7
examples of the Fokker D.XXI fighter were bought, and
manufacturing licences for both the D.XXI and C.X
were acquired, followed in April 1938 by one for the
Blenheim. 30 C.Xs were delivered in 1938, and in
October of that year the first D.XXI came off the line.
At the same time the system of semi-autonomous Flight
Stations with attached units ended, and a number of
Flight Regiments (Lentorymentti) were formed, the air
force being reorganised as follows:—

Air Force Headquarters, Helsinki.
LeR 1, H.Q. at Suur-Merijoki, four ground liaison
squadrons, TLeLv (Tiedustelulaivue) 10, 12, 14 and
16 at Viipuri and Sortavala.
LeR 2, H.Q. at Utti, two fighter squadrons, HLeLv
(Hävittäjälentolaivue) 24 and 26 at Utti.
LeR 4, H.Q. at Immola, two squadrons for long range
missions, PLeLv (Pommituslentolaivue) 44 and 46 at
Immola in the Valley of Vuoksi.
Detached squadron for maritime duties, TLeLv 36 at
Santahamina.
Military School of Aviation at Kauhava.
School of Mechanics at Santahamina.
Air Force Depot at Tampere.

By the autumn of 1939, these squadrons were disposed
and equipped as follows:—
TLeLv 10: 12 Fokker C.X at Lappeenranta for dive-
bombing.
TLeLv 12: 13 Fokker C.Xs at Suur-Merijoki for reconnaissance and co-operation with II Army Corps in the
Western Isthmus of Karelia.
TLeLv 14: Fokker C.VEs and 4 C.Xs at Laikko for
reconnaissance and co-operation with III Army Corps
in the Eastern Isthmus of Karelia.
TLeLv 16: 9 Blackburn Ripon IIFs and 5 Junkers K43s,
the two flights of Ripons at Wärtsila for operations over

north-east Lake Ladoga, one flight of K.43s in Nor-
thern Finland.
HLeLv 24: 36 Fokker D.XXIs at Immola.
HLeLv 26: 10 Bristol Bulldog IVAs at Raulampi.
PLeLv 44: 8 Bristol Blenheim Is at Luonetjarvi.
PLeLv 46: 6 Bristol Blenheim Is and 3 Avro Ansons Is
at Luonetjarvi.
TLeLv 36: 6 Blackburn Ripon IIFs at Kallvik.
TLeLv 39: 2 Junkers K.43s — from TLeLv 16 — just
forming at Mariehamm, Aland.

In addition, a contract had been signed with the
Italian Fiat organisation for the supply of 35 G.50 fighters,
but none had yet arrived. The 9 remaining Gamecock IIs
recently replaced in HLeLv 24, were still in use for
advanced training alongside many other types. Total
strength was 145 aircraft of which 114 were airworthy.

This then, was the position in November 1939 when
the Russians, having demanded with increasing forceful-
ness, facilities for military installations and airfields in
Finland for the defence of Leningrad, fabricated a border
incident and on 30th, invaded. The Russian ground forces
were supported by some 900 aircraft, but, expecting no
real opposition from the Finns, many of these were
obsolescent. The first air action took place on 1 December, when Lt. Eino Luukkanen of HLeLv 24 intercepted
two Tupolev SB 2s and shot down one. Bad weather
prevented much flying for the rest of the month, but
in January it was possible to get into the air more, and
on 6th two D.XXIs of HLeLv 24 intercepted 7 Ilyushin
DB-3 bombers, shooting down all of them, Capt. Jorma
Sarvanto claiming 6 and Capt. Per-Erik Sovelius one.

The overwhelming strength of the Red Air Force
prevented supression of its activities, but such grievous
losses were inflicted that more modern types were rushed
to the front, bringing committed strength to an estimated
1,500. The preponderance of Russian aircraft in the sky
caused the reconnaissance and bombing squadrons to
have to fly most of their missions at dusk, or during
the night. Late in December the first 2 Fiat G-50s had
arrived, but the rest were delayed crossing Germany.
Help was on the way however, as the gallant fight put
up by the Finns had gained them much sympathy
throughout the Western world. On 11 January 1940 a
complete wing of Swedish volunteers with aircraft from
the Swedish Air Force, Flygflottilj 19 (numbered by the
Finns LeR 19), equipped with 12 J 8 Gloster Gladiator
Is and 4 Hawker Swedish-Harts, led by Major Hugo
Beckhammar, arrived in Northern Finland to fly from
the frozen Lake Kemi. Operating separately from the
main Finnish air forces, the Swedes were forced to split
up into small detachments following bombing attacks on
their base, but by the end of the fighting when they
returned home they had shot down 6 fighters and 6
bombers, including a four-engined TB-3 for the loss of
3 Gladiators and 3 Harts, all flying having taken place in
appalling weather conditions.

In December France began shipping 30 Morane 406
fighters as a gift, while in Great Britain 30 Gladiator IIs
and 24 Gloster Gauntlet IIs were taken out of storage at
a Maintenance Unit, the Gauntlets and 10 of the Gladia-

Junkers K.43 bomber-floatplane of LLv 44 at Viipuri, Lentoasema 6.   (E. Ritaranta).

I.V.L. A.22 (Hansa-Brandenburg W.33) licence-built in Finland. This aircraft is 4E17.   (E. Ritaranta).

tors being given to the Finns, the other 20 Gladiators and 12 Bristol Blenheim IVs being sold to them. All but one of the Blenheims arrived safely and were issued to PLeLv 44, this unit passing 5 of its Mark Is to PLeLv 44 to make good losses. Late in January 12 of the Gladiators were given to HLeLv 26 to replace this unit's Bulldogs which had managed to shoot down one SB-2 up to this time, and early in February another 18 Gladiators were sent to the squadron. Although initially liked by the pilots due to their handling qualities, the Gladiators lacked armour protection and self-sealing tanks, and when in action against I-16s and I-153s were soon in trouble, 13 being lost by the end of February.

Meantime, the Moranes were used to form a new squadron, HLeLv 28, under Major Jusu; although initially the engine cannons were not available, the aircraft went into action during February, mainly in a ground strafing role. 22 of the Gauntlets, unsuitable for operational use, and the Bulldogs which had been replaced by the Gladiators, were used for operational training, joined by 3 J-6A Jaktfalk fighters sent to Finland by the Swedes. 3 Fokker C.VDs were also sent from Sweden, and were delivered to TLeLv 16, 2 Koolhoven FK-52 two-seat fighters being passed to TLeLv 36, while a single Douglas DC-2 was converted for use as a bomber; named " Hanssin Jukka ", the aircraft saw a little action in this role before reverting to transport duties.

At last the Fiat G-50s began to arrive, and late in February the first 14 went to HLeLv 26 to replace the disappointing Gladiators, 8 of which were handed to TLeLv 12 and 6 to TLeLv 14 for fighter-reconnaissance duties; in March 12 more G-50s were delivered, the squadron being reported to have entered action during March. 12 more Blenheim Is were purchased from Great Britain during February, a third bomber squadron, PLeLv 42 being formed, and from America 44 Brewster 239s, surplus to U.S. Navy requirements, were ordered, and the first few arrived.

A large number of foreign volunteer pilots had come to Finland, the first of these, all Danish, having been posted to HLeLv 24. Now, late in February the others, Danes, Poles, Americans, Canadians, Italians, Spaniards and British, were formed into a special unit, HLeLv 22 under Capt. Erkki at Hollola, and these were to have the Brewsters, but only 6 had been received by the Armistice, when the unit was disbanded and the volunteers left for home.

During the fighting the Finns found their fighters were well able to deal with the Polikarpov I-15 and I-15bis biplane fighters, but the I-153 and I-16s were much more formidable opponents. Despite this, the success of the Finnish pilots was most noteable, 200 confirmed and 80 unconfirmed victories being claimed for the loss of 67 aircraft, 42 in action, 69 more being damaged. A further 314 enemy aircraft were claimed by the anti-aircraft gunners and 90 more to other causes, while 105 were believed to have been destroyed on the ground in bombing and strafing attacks.

While the Gladiators had suffered most, the Blenheims had also had a number of losses, 4 of the Mark IVs being

destroyed and 3 damaged by the end of January, but the most successful aircraft had proved to be the Fokker D.XXIs and C.Xs. Amongst the pilots, those of HLeLv 24 were supreme, Capt. Sarvanto having been credited with 13 victories, mainly bombers, and nine other pilots claimed 5 or more victories, Flt.Mstr. Viktori Pyötsiä having 7½, Capt. Per-Erik Sovelius and Flt. Mstr. Kelpo Virta 7 each; among these 10 pilots, three had been killed, Sgt. Pentti Tilli (5 victories) on 19 January 1940 when he was shot down by six Russian fighters, Lt. Jaakko Vuorela (6 victories) on 30 January, and Lt. Tatu Huhanantti (6 victories) when on 28 February, after being wounded in action, he rammed a Russian fighter. Two Danish volunteers in the unit also did well, J. Ulrich getting 3 and E. Frijs 2. In HLeLv 26, Flt.Mstr. Oiva Tuominen was outstanding, with 8 victories while flying Gladiators, Lt. Urko Nieminen claiming 5 and Capt. Risto Puhakka 4.

During the final stages of the Winter War practically all units were concentrated to support the army fighting round Viipuri, strafing Soviet troops advancing over the frozen Gulf of Finland, and by this time the Russian air strength had grown to over 2,000; on 13 March 1940 the gallant Finns were forced to accept an armistice, a considerable area of the country being ceded to the Soviet Union. By this date the number of operational aircraft available had risen to 196, but of these, only 112 were serviceable (see Appendices).

The Finns were now given a breathing space, but it was clear that the Armistice had done little to erase tension, and every effort was made to modernise and expand the air force as quickly as possible. Early in 1940 the State Aircraft Factory completed its batch of 35 D.XXIs and began overhauling the various aircraft damaged in the recent fighting. By May, 6 Caudron C.714 fighters had arrived from France as a gift, and 12 Hawker Hurricane Is were purchased from Great Britain; 11 of these were flown over by Finnish pilots, one being lost en route, when it crashed in Norway, and the twelfth was delivered by sea. Ten Westland Lysander Is and one Mark II were also delivered.

The fall of Norway brought 7 Norwegian Air Force aircraft, which flew to Finland to escape capture and were interned, and these, a Heinkel He 115A-2 and 3 Høver MF 11 floatplanes, 2 Fokker C.VDs and a De Havilland Tiger Moth, were all pressed into service. The fall of Holland during the same month however, prevented delivery of 26 Fokker G-IB twin-engined fighters and 5 T-VIIIL bombers, which had been ordered, and which were now taken over by the occupying Germans. Meanwhile, the pilots of HLeLv 24 had been fetching the rest of the Brewster 239s to the country, these having been off-loaded and erected in Sweden. On completion of delivery, these aircraft were taken on strength by this crack unit, its D.XXIs being released for the formation of new squadrons.

Joined by the newly-completed D.XXIs from the factory, these latter were initially issued to form HLeLv 30, the personnel for this squadron coming from TLeLv 10, the dive-bomber unit, which was disbanded; the Hurri-

Breguet XIV A–2 of the Ground Reconnaissance Squadron with Flg.Div.1 at Utti.   (E. Ritaranta).

canes and C. 714s were also taken on charge, though the French aircraft were soon discarded aas unsuitable for use from Finnish airfields. More D.XXIs went to form HLeLv 32, and later in the year a new regiment, LeR 3, was formed at Pori on the west coast, to incorporate these two units. A number of Russian Tupolev SB 2 and 2bis aircraft which had crash-landed in Finland during the war were repaired, and 6 of these were used for the formation of a new sea reconnaissance squadron, TLeLv 6, which was formed from the disbanded TLeLv 36, taking over that unit's remaining Ripon IIs also, and the Norwegian Høver MF 11s.

On completion of the repair work, the State Aircraft Factory began production again in 1941, setting up lines for the D.XXI, Blenheim I, and home-designed V.L. Pyry II advanced trainer, an aircraft very similar in appearance to the D.XXI. Shortage of Mercury engines, which were required for the Blenheims particularly, led to the decision to modify the D.XXIs to take the 825 h.p. Pratt and Whitney Twin Wasp Jr. engine, which was being manufactured in Sweden without licence. Some re-design of the nose and tail was necessary, the whole armament being moved to the wings, and the cockpit glazing was also extended to provide a better view; regrettably, the resulting aircraft did not possess quite the performance of the original Mercury-powered version, but nonetheless 50 were produced during the year, as well as 15 Blenheim Is and 40 Pyry IIs.

Seeing Finland as a potential future ally for the secretly-planned invasion of Russia, and wanting harbour and transport facilities in the country for their forces in Norway, the Germans now offered to sell the Finns some of the aircraft taken by them as war booty during 1940, and these were gladly accepted. Twenty-five ex-Armee de l'Air Morane 406s and 22 Curtiss Hawk 75A-3s, together with 7 ex-Norwegian Hawk 75A-6s, all of which had been overhauled and fitted with German instruments, were purchased, as were 4 Dornier Do 22K-1 floatplanes of obscure origin.

On arrival, the Do 22s were issued to TLeLv 6, and the Hawk 75A-6s, which arrived some while before the 75A-3, went to TLeLv 14 for fighter-reconnaissance duties, the Moranes being used for the reinforcement of HLeLv 28 as necessary. A certain amount of re-equipment and re-distribution of equipment within the reconnaissance and ground support units also took place, and when Germany invaded the Soviet Union on 22 June 1941, the Finnish air force order of battle was as follows:

LeR 1

TLeLv 12: One flight of Mercury-D.XXIs, one flight of Twin Wasp Jr.-D.XXIs, one flight of 8 Fokker C.Xs.

TLeLv 14: 6 Curtiss Hawk 75A-6s, and various Fokker biplanes.

TLeLv 16: One flight of Fokker C.Xs, one flight of Westland Lysanders, one flight of Gloster Gladiator IIs.

LeR 2

HLeLv 24: 40 Brewster 239s.

HLeLv 26: 25 Fiat G.50s.

HLeLv 28: 29 Morane 406s.

LeR 3

HLeLv 30: One flight of Hawker Hurricane Is, one flight of Mercury-D.XXIs.

HLeLv 32: 17 Mercury-D.XXIs, 19 Twin Wasp Jr.-D.XXIs.

LeR 4

PLeLv 42: 9 Bristol Blenheim Is.

PLeLv 44: 9 Bristol Blenheim Is.

PLeLv 46: 6 Bristol Blenheim Is and 3 Bristol Blenheim IVs.

Autonomous

TLeLv 6: 6 Tupolev SB-2s and SB-2bis's, 3 Høver MF 11s, a number of Blackburn Ripon IIs.

Total strength of the air force was 550 aircraft of which over half were operational types.

On 25 June 1941, the Russians, desirous of protecting their borders against further unexpected attacks, began bombing raids over the Finnish border, these bringing Finland into what was to be known in that country as the Continuation War: the first such raid was intercepted by the Mercury-powered D.XXIs of HLeLv 32, and two DB-3s were shot down. As a result of the fighting on other fronts in Central and Southern Russia only a relatively small air force could be maintained by the Russians in the north, and that was initially equipped mainly with obsolescent types; as a result the conflict in the first months was far more equal than in 1940, and the Finns soon gained a considerable ascendency in the air.

Shortage of Russian aircraft prevented bombing raids being mounted against Finnish towns as they had been in the Winter War, and relieved therefore of the necessity to retain a large part of the fighter force for home defence, most Finnish units were able to move up to the front, attacking enemy ground forces and escorting bombers. The first Finnish offensive began south of Lake Ladoga, and

Martinsyde F.4 Buzzard, used for fighter training.   (E. Ritaranta).

Caudron C.59 trainer, coded 2E5. Note Gourdou-Lesurre GL–21 fighter in the background, featuring colourful fuselage band. (E. Ritaranta).

the territory ceded to Russia was soon recaptured. Despite German pressure however, the Finns refused to take part in the attack on Leningrad and after a short concentration on the Karelian Isthmus, forces were shifted north of the Lake for a push into Russian East Karelia, the intention being to try and cut the Murmansk railway down which Lease-Lend supplies from America and Great Britain were pouring from the port of Archangel. This thrust was accompanied by a German one from Northern Norway, the two armies being eventually intended to link up, but late in the year the Finns were held at the town of Petroskoi, and the two armies were destined never to link and complete their giant pincer movement.

In November traffic on the Murmansk railway was within range of air attack by fighters, and HLeLv 28 was ordered to the Petroskoi area, the cannon armament of the Moranes making them particularly suitable for " train busting," a task in which they were joined by the Blenheims of PLeLv 42 and 44; PLeLv 46 at this time operated mainly in the photographic reconnaissance role, and also ferried in fuel supplies to the forces assaulting the Petroskoi defences.

Early in the campaign, HLeLv 32 had exchanged 11 of its Mercury-D.XXIs for TLeLv 14's 6 Hawk 75A-6s, and when the Hawk 75A-3s were ready for service they were delivered to this former unit, which was fully-equipped with the Curtiss aircraft by August 1941. There was considerable air combat during the first months of the war, but once the front stabilized in Eastern Karelia, trench warfare not unlike that of the First World War developed, and opposition declined considerably, the Finns being able to redistribute air force units, and make good attrition. To help in this the Germans began selling them Russian war material captured during their advance in the Ukraine. The Finns already had a number of SB-2s and SB-2bis's, as has already been recounted, together with some I-15bis, I-153, I-16 and DB-3 aircraft, and more I-153s, SB-2bis's and DB-3s were supplied. The Hurricane Is were reduced by attrition to only 6 aircraft by this time, and these were released for home defence duties, their place being taken in one flight of HLeLv 30 by the I-153s. The Lysanders had been reduced to only 5 aircraft, and were taken out of front line service.

During November 1941 a fourth bomber squadron, PLeLv 48, began forming; in December LeR 1 was disbanded and the close support squadrons were attached to the various army formations with which they were flying. In the Spring of 1942 as it became clear that further fluid warfare was unlikely for some time, it was decided to form mixed regiments to support various sectors of the front, and on 3 May LeR 1 was re-activated to cover the Isthmus of Aunus, with TLeLv 12, equipped with both Mercury- and Twin Wasp Jr.-powered D.XXIs, TLeLv 14 with D.XXIs and Fokker C.VEs, and by HLeLv 32 from LeR 3, with 13 Hawks. This latter unit set up base at Nurmoila, and was very active on the Syväri River front during the summer, suffering attrition until few aircraft were left on hand.

LeR 2 was to take over the Onega and Maaselkä area, and incorporated TLeLv 16 and HLeLv 28, the latter continuing the attacks on the Murmansk railway. LeR 3 was to cover the Karelian Isthmus with HLeLvs 24, 26 and 30, the latter unit now becoming a reconnaissance and close support unit, Twin Wasp Jr.-D.XXIs having replaced the Mercury-powered version, and I-153s the Hurricanes. LeR 4 remained responsible for long-range reconnaissance and bombing duties on all fronts. This regiment received reinforcements in early 1942 when 15 Dornier Do 17Z-2 bombers, a gift from Reischmarshal Hermann Goering, arrived and were issued to PLeLv 46, the latter unit passing its Blenheim Is and IVs to PLeLv 48, though this unit was still not fully operational for some time.

The lack of activity in the air during early 1942 allowed a lot of training to be carried out, and efforts were also made to improve the radio control and direction of fighters in the air — one of the weakest points in the Finnish air force — in order to make them more effective. In November 1942 a fifth regiment, LeR 5, was formed for operations over Southern Finland and the Finnish Bay; this regiment took on strength TLeLv 6, and TLeLv 14 from LeR 1, TLeLv 30 following later from LeR 3. This latter unit was by that date fully equipped with I-153s, 21 of which had been received. Other Russian aircraft received around this time from the Germans included 3 LaGG-3 fighters, which went to HLeLv 32 where they were used for high speed reconnaissance; 4 Beriev MBR-2 flying-boats were used by TLeLv 12, and the total number of SB-2 and SB-2bis aircraft received totalled 24; one of these aircraft had the sinking of no less than four Russian submarines to its credit, a fair indication of the good use to which they were put. 11 DB-3s and 4 DB-3Fs were divided between PLeLv 46 and 48, and a number of Pe-2s and 2FTs were issued to PLeLv 48 to form a long-range reconnaissance flight.

More aircraft were delivered in 1943; early in the year

Polyanvirta reconnaissance-bomber. (E. Ritaranta).

Martinsyde Buzzard fighter-trainer marked with later-style codes. See colour illustration. (E. Ritaranta).

the Germans supplied 12 more Hawk 75A-3s from France, followed by another 3 in 1944, to make good the attrition suffered by HLeLv 32, and these were followed by 32 more Moranes, including some MS 410s, fitted with four belt-fed wing machine-guns in place of the pair of drum-fed machine-guns of the MS 406. Eighty-seven of the French aircraft had now been received, and over the next year it was to be the most numerous type on strength. Also in the Spring 23 Junkers Ju 88A-4s arrived, and these replaced the Blenheims in PLeLv 44. During the year the State Aircraft Factory began delivering a further 30 Blenheim Is, PLeLv 42 being brought up to strength, as was PLeLv 48, which at last became fully-operational.

During the latter months of 1942 more modern Russian aircraft such as the LaGG-3 and Yak-1 and 7 had been appearing in northern skies, together with Lend-Lease types such as the Hawker Hurricane II, Bell P-39 Airacobra and Curtiss P-40, but the quality of training of the Soviet pilots remained low, allowing the highly-experienced Finns, whose morale was extremely good, to prevent the superior performance of the enemy's aircraft from overwhelming them, but nonetheless the Finnish air supremacy began to falter. In 1943 not only did the even better La-5 and Yak-9 fighters begin being met, but the quality of the Russian pilots became noticeably higher. With the promise from the Germans of more modern fighters to meet this threat, LeR 3 began forming a new fighter squadron, HLeLv 34, in January 1943, and in March, 16 Messerschmitt Bf 109G-2s arrived to equip this. In order to make the best possible use of the new aircraft, several of the most outstanding pilots from the other squadrons were selected to fly them.

Up to this time the Brewster 239 had proved to be the supreme fighter at the front, the 239 model possessing far greater sensitivity of control and manoeuvreability than the later models which had such a disastrous career with the British, Dutch and Americans in the Pacific. Possibly a good deal of this success was due to the fact that the pilots of HLeLv 24 were the most experienced in the air force at the start of the Continuation War, having the whole of the Winter War fighting on D.XXIs behind them to draw upon. Outstanding among this unit's pilots in early 1943 was Eino Juutilainen, who had claimed 28 victories since 25 June 1941 to bring his total score to 30; on one occasion, while on a lone reconnaissance flight, he had encountered 22 Russian fighters and shot down 3 of them.

In the same unit at this time were Jorma Karhunen, who had added 21 victories to his Winter War score of 4, and Lauri Nissinen who added 19 to an earlier score of 5; both were holders of the Mannerheim Cross. Eero Kinnunen had claimed 19 to add to a 1940 score of $3\frac{1}{2}$, but had been killed on 21 April 1943; Eino Luukanen, who was to finish the war as the country's third-ranking ace, had gained 16 victories with the Brewster before a posting to command TLeLv 30 in late 1942 had temporarily put an end to his fighting career, and another pilot, Nils Katajainen, had done well also until unaccountably posted to fly SB-2s in TLeLv 6. Another young Brewster pilot building up a big score was Hans Wind, who had already shot down 3 aircraft in a day on three occasions, and was to receive his first Mannerheim Cross in July. Many other pilots in HLeLv 24 were also doing well.

The Curtiss Hawk had also put up a good performance, and was well-liked, being rugged and manoeuvreable; Flt.Mstr. Eino Koskinen was to gain 11 victories on this type before being killed in an accident in 1944, and Lt. Kossi Karhila had got 10 before he was posted to HLeLv 34 in Spring 1943. Other successful pilots were Lt. Jaakko Hillo with 9, and Capt. Paavo Berg who had shot down 7 during the first campaigns of the war, before being killed on 1 November 1941. Four other pilots also claimed 7 with the Hawk. The Morane 406, though giving some trouble with its electrical systems, and although used to a large extent for ground attack work, had nevertheless given a good account of itself, proving superior to the I-16 and able to outmanoeuvre the LaGG-3. Sgt. Toivo Tomminen shot down 6 Russian aircraft in the early months of the Continuation War, before being killed in December 1941, while Aatto Laikinen and Urho Lehtovaara each claimed 10, Lehtovaara then going to HLeLv 34 and Laikinen being killed in June 1944. Other successful Morane pilots included Lars Hattinen, who claimed 6, Paavo Myllylä and Antti Tani, both the latter later serving in HLeLv 34.

The least successful of the main fighter types had been the Fiat G-50s, which had given much trouble during the winter cold, and which were somewhat under-armed. Despite this, in Spring 1943 Oiva Tuominen had gained 22 victories on this type to add to the 8 he had claimed in 1940 while flying Gladiators, to equal Juutilainen's score of 30, and make him one of Finland's two top aces at this stage. He had also been the first fighter pilot to receive the Mannerheim Cross, which he was awarded for shooting down 4 bombers in four minutes on 17 August 1941. Risto Puhakka also did well on the Fiat before he and Tuominen joined HLeLv 34, and so did Klaus Alakoski, while Lauri Lantamäki and J. Hämäläinen stayed with the squadron until the end, claiming

Gourdou-Leseurre GL-21 of the Utti Fighter Squadron of Flg.Div.1. This was Finland's only fighter unit throughout the twenties. The aircraft is coded GL-11. (E. Ritaranta).

Line of floatplanes on the edge of a typical Finnish lake. The nearest aircraft is a V.L.Saaski II (SA–125), then come two A–22s, and furthest away are a pair of V.L.Kotka IIs (KA–146 and 148) (E. Ritaranta).

5 each. One of the ingredients of the Finns' success had been the way in which they had been able to split their rather large fighter squadrons into flights of 10 or a dozen aircraft, which had operated from airfields wherever they were needed, rather than being concentrated at a small number of major bases.

Thus in March 1943 HLeLv 34 began to receive its Bf 109G-2s, but soon after their arrival, Maj. Olavi Ehrenrooth, who had been posted from commanding HLeLv 32 to lead this new unit, was killed in an accident in a Pyry trainer, and Maj. Eino Luukkanen was posted from TLeLv 30 to take his place. A little later Maj. G. E. Magnusson, commander of HLeLv 24, and Finland's " grand old man " of the fighters, was promoted to Lt. Col. and given command of LeR3, the squadron being taken over by Jorma Karhunen. The Messerschmitts of HLeLv 34 went into action in May 1943, and at once began a considerable run of successes, being reinforced during the summer by a further 32 aircraft.

During the late summer 14 of the third batch of Morane 406s were supplied to TLeLv 14 for fighter-reconnaissance duties, and some Bf 109G-2s were supplied to TLeLv 30. This squadron's I-153s had given some trouble due to the unreliability of their engines, and a number of pilots had been lost due to engine failures. The bombers of the four squadrons of LeR4 had concentrated throughout the fighting on immediate tactical targets close to the front, but on 19 September 1943 one attempt was made at a full scale strategic raid, the target being Lavansaari Island in the Gulf of Finland. 14 Ju 88s, 6 Do 17s, 6 Blenheims and 4 DB-3s set out, but soon after take off the weather deteriorated greatly, and many of the bombers became lost; as a result the raid was something of a shambles, few aircraft reaching the target, and many 'carrying out forced landings at other bases on the way home, one aircraft crashing, one belly-landing and one being abandoned by its crew.

The State Aircraft Factory continued turning out new aircraft, overhauling and repairing existing ones, and also doing a considerable amount of design and development work. During 1944 10 Blenheim IVs were produced, together with 4 more D.XXIs and 4 C.Xs. A D.XXI had been experimentally fitted with a retractable undercarriage, but the resulting increase in performance was not good enough to warrant production. Development therefore took place of a home-designed fighter to replace the D.XXI in production, the first example of the V.L. Myrsky flying in 1942; following protracted teething troubles, the Mark II version of the aircraft was finally put into production, and deliveries began during 1944. A further development was an all-wood copy of the Brewster 239, powered by a 1,000 h.p. Russian M-63 radial engine, known as the Humu; one example was completed, but the aircraft did not enter production.

Less ambitious but extremely effective was a project to prolong the life of the Morane 406; the fighter's 860 h.p. Hispano Suiza 12Y-31 engine had also been licence-manufactured in Russia, and the Klimov M105P of 1,150 h.p., fitted to the LaGG-3, was a development of this. Quantities of the Russian engine had been captured by the Germans, and with only slight modification of the nose contours, engine cowling and oil cooler intakes, these were fitted in the Moranes. The loss of the 20 mm. " moteur-cannon " of the 12Y-31 was initally made good by fitting a German MG 151 cannon, but the weight of this added to the heavier engine, upset the aircraft's centre of gravity. Supplies of the MG 151 were in any case dubious, and numbers of the captured Russian Beresin 12.7 mm. B.S. machine-gun were available. This was an exteremely efficient weapon, lighter, and in many ways superior to the 20 mm. gun, and this was successfully fitted in the hollow propeller shaft of the M105P. These alterations in no way reduced the Morane's good handling qualities, but raised the maximum speed to 326 m.p.h., giving it a definite edge over the LaGG-3. As aircraft were due for major overhaul, they were called in to the factory and modified in this way, the first examples of the Mörkö-Moranni, as it was known, being returned to HLeLv 28 in the early summer of 1944.

In April 1944 the first examples of the Messerschmitt Bf 109G-6 were delivered from Germany, and were issued to HLeLv 34. This unit's surviving G-2s were passed to HLeLv 24, and at the same time TLeLv 30 disbanded, passing its G-2s to this unit also, giving it a total of 15. On arrival the first of the new G-6s were fitted with three 20 mm. cannons, but the extra pair of underwing guns so impaired the fighter's performance that the Finns soon had them removed. The extra guns had mainly been

V.L. D.27 Haukka II fighter. This is one of two examples of the Haukka II produced by the State Aircraft Factory. (E. Ritaranta).

Fokker C.VE reconnaissance-bomber of LLv 12, at Suur-Merijoki with Lentoasema 5 during the early thirties. (G. H. Kamphuis).

fitted for attacks on American four-engined bombers over Germany, and against all Russian aircraft except the heavily-armoured Il-2s, were not really necessary, good performance being more important in the face of the large numbers of nimble Russian fighters. During the same month TLeLv's long-serving Fokker C.Xs were withdrawn and replaced by Blenheim Is. In early June more Bf 109G-6s arrived (a total of 114 were to be received altogether); some of these were issued to HLeLv 24, the G-2s then going to equip one flight of HLeLv 28, the other being fully re-equipped with Mörkö-Morannis. HLeLv 24's faithful but tired and depleted Brewsters were passed to HLeLv 26, and the latter's G-50s were removed from front line service, going instead to the operational training units.

As the Spring ended and the Summer approached, the air force comprised five Flight Regiments containing six fighter squadrons, four reconnaissance and four bombing squadrons, and also a flying division for the evacuation of wounded and supply transportation, flying a variety of liaison and transport aircraft, including five Luftwaffe aircraft on loan, 2 He 115s, 2 He 59s and a Fw. Weihe. This force included well over 200 fighters and more than 100 bombers. (See Appendices.)

LeR 1
TLeLv 12: Two flights of Fokker D.XXIs, one flight of Bristol Blenheim Is.
HLeLv 32: Curtiss Hawk 75As, 3 LaGG-3s and 1 Curtiss Kittyhawk (captured from the Russians, but not flown on operations).

LeR 2
TLeLv 16: Fokker C.Xs and Gloster Gladiator IIs.
HLeLv 28: One flight of Mörkö-Morannis and one flight of Messerschmitt Bf 109G-2s.

LeR 3
HLeLv 24: Messerschmitt Bf 109G-6s.
HLeLv 26: Brewster 239s.
HLeLv 34: Messerschmitt Bf 109G-6s.

LeR 4
PLeLv 42: 18 Bristol Blenheim Is.
PLeLv 44: Junkers Ju 88A-4s.
PLeLv 46: 9 Dornier Do 17Z-2s, 2 DB-3s and 3 DB-3Fs.
PLeLV 48: 19 Bristol Blenheim Is and IVs and 3 Pe-2s.

LeR 5
TLeLv 6: Tupolev SB-2s and SB-2bis's, Dornier Do 22K-1s and Høver MF 11s.
TLeLv 14: Morane 406s and Fokker D.XXIs.

In the summer of 1944, having sent the German armies in central and southern Russia reeling back, the Russians were at last able to launch a full scale offensive in the north. This began in mid June, and was launched with overwhelming forces, and suddenly the position was again as it had been in the Winter of 1939/40. Battling against tremendous odds in the air and on the ground, the Finns put up an epic resistance, but all efforts could only delay the inevitable in the face of the massive power thrown against them. All of a sudden the fighter pilots found themselves in a position similar to that which the Germans further south had been in for many months, and with unlimited targets to choose from, squadron and individual scores rocketted. Between 1 June and 5 August HLeLv 24 claimed 240 confirmed victories, 33 probables and 32 damaged, a better performance even than the unit had put up in the Winter War; in HLeLv 34 Maj. Luukkanen, who between December 1939 and May 1944 had claimed 34 victories, now claimed 20 more between 14 June and 5 August, while Flt.Mstr. Juutilainen's score reached a fantastic 94 without his own aircraft ever being struck by an enemy bullet, and Flt.Mstr. Nils Katajainen, back on operations with fighters, shot down 18 aircraft in 10 days during this period.

In the face of the Russian's overwhelming superiority in numbers, the Finns quickly gave up the Karelian Isthmus positions and withdrew to the hill of Viipuri where a defence could be better maintained, at the same time retiring from Eastern Karelia to behind the former

V.L. Kotka floatplane, probably from LLv 38 at Sortavala, in the early thirties. (E. Ritaranta).

Caudron C.60 basic trainer. The aircraft is coded CA–33. (E. Ritaranta).

state frontiers in the north. The Viipuri position was held for a while, but once the Russians battered their way through the defences all was lost, and on 4 September 1944 an armistice was again accepted.

Early in August TLeLv 12 was re-equipped with Myrsky IIs, 47 of which were produced in 1944, but these had little chance to show their worth, claiming just 6 victories before the end of the fighting. They were not, however, outstandingly successful in service. By the end of the fighting the Finns had claimed a further 1,567 air victories since 1941, 550 of them during 1944, losing 536 aircraft, 209 of them on operations; of 155 pilots who claimed any enemy aircraft destroyed, no less than 87 were credited with 5 or more victories. Bomber losses during the final campaign had been heavy, but the fighters had performed prodigious feats. As already mentioned, Juutilainen's score had risen to 94, and in HLeLv 24 Capt. Hans Wind had 78; both pilots had been twice awarded the Mannerheim Cross. Also in HLeLv 24 Nils Katajainen had brought his score to 36, Kauko Puro to 35, Lauri Nissinen to $32\frac{1}{2}$ and Jorma Karhunen to 31, while in HLeLv 34 Maj Luukkanen had 54, Urho Lehtovaara 44, Risto Puhakka and Oiva Tuominen 43 each, and Kyösti Karhila $29\frac{1}{2}$; all these pilots with the exception of Nissinen had survived. Seven more pilots had scores of 20 or higher, four of them in HLeLv 24 and three in HLeLv 34; two of these had been killed, only one in the recent fighting.

The State Aircraft Factory, which had repaired or renewed 600 aircraft during the war, and produced 200 more, had continued development right to the last, building a refined version of the Myrsky fitted with a Daimler-Benz DB 605AC inline engine of 1,475 h.p., known as the Pyörremyrsky, but only one had been completed by the Armistice. The fighting was still not over for the Finns however, as one term of the Armistice required the removal from Northern Finland of the German forces operating there. These were not prepared to go without a stubborn fight, and the Finns were forced to drive them slowly out of Finnish Lapland and into Northern Norway, the Germans comprehensively dynamiting all villages and towns, bridges and other structures as they went. Due to a scarcity of bases in this area, the Bf 109Gs did not have the range to take part, and the older types were generally used to support the army, TLeLv 12 and 16, HLeLvs 26, 28 and 32 and PLeLv 42, 44, 46 and 48 taking part in these actions, Myrskys, Fokker C.Xs, Brewster 239s, Mörkö-Morannis, Hawks, Blenheims, Ju 88s, Do 17Zs, DB-3s and DB-3Fs being used. The Germans did not offer any considerable air opposition,

but their flak was accurate and intense, taking a heavy toll of the aircraft harrying them, 17 being lost during this period. Air operations generally were confined to the capture of certain towns and important roads, and continued until 25 April 1945. By late January the squadrons were back at their peacetime bases, from where they continued operations, but meanwhile in December 1944, a complete renumbering of units took place.

By this date LeR 5 had been disbanded as had several squadrons, TLeLv 6 and 14, HLeLv 32 and PLeLv 48 being no more, though the Hawks of the fighter unit had gone to TLeLv 16 where they had first begun service in 1941. The renumbering was as follows:—

LeR 1 at Pori
TLeLv 12 became HLeLv 11: Myrsky IIs.
TLeLv 16 became HLeLv 13: Curtiss Hawk 75As.
LeR 2 at Rissala
HLeLv 26 became HLeLv 21: Brewster 239s.
HLeLv 28 became HLeLv 23: Mörkö-Morannis.
LeR 3 at Utti
HLeLv 24 became HLeLv 31: Messerschmitt Bf 109G-6s.
HLeLv 34 became HLeLv 33: Messerschmitt Bf 109G-6s.
LeR 4 at Luonetjarvi
PLeLv 42 became PLeLv 41: Bristol Blenheims.
PLeLv 44 became PLeLv 43: Junkers Ju 88A-4s.
PLeLv46 becaame PLeLv 45: Dornier Do 17Z-2s.

All Russian types such as I-153s, SB-2s and DB-3s had been sent to the Air Force base at Tampere for disposition by the Allied Armistice Commission. Most squadrons were under strength and the only aircraft of which adequate replacements were available in store was the Bf 109G-6. During the winter of 1946/7 the unpopular Myrskys were phased out of service, and were replaced by the former aircraft, and other Messerschmitts went to the bomber units as cannibalisation and accidents reduced their strength.

On 10 February 1947 the Peace Treaty was finally signed in Paris, and this limited the Finns to an air force with an operational strength of 60 aircraft and staffed by 3,000 personnel. No aircraft with internal bomb loading were to be used, and no missiles or nuclear weapons were to be allowed. This, and the heavy reparations the Finns were obliged to pay to the Russians, resulted in no re-equipment taking place for some years, and consequently to a depression in the national aircraft industry.

The following year the Ju 88s and Do 17s were withdrawn, PLeLv 43 and 45 being disbanded, and the Hawks also went, though HLeLv 13 was re-equipped with Bf 109G-6s. A hundred of these were still available, so it was decided to standardise on the aircraft, and although LeR 2 retained its Brewsters and Mörkö-Morannis for several more years, these were only employed for training.

In 1951 sufficient money was at last available for some

Licence-built Letov S.128 Smolik primary trainer. (E. Ritaranta).

Aero A–11 reconnaissance-bomber of the Detached Ground Flight Squadron at Suur-Merijoki, about 1930. (E. Ritaranta).

new equipment, and the State Aircraft Factory was requested to design a new advanced trainer to provide also interim equipment for some of the units, the Vihuri being produced and ordered. 1952 saw a complete reorganisation when the Flight Regiments were disbanded and replaced by wings (Lennosto), the squadrons also being renamed Hävittäjälaivue. LeR 2 was disbanded completely, the surviving Mörkö-Morannis and Brewsters

HävLv 11. In the meantime the Bf 109G-6s soldiered on until 1954 when they were finally withdrawn, and in 1955 a further order with De Havillands brought 4 Vampire T.55s to Finland for jet conversion training, later to be followed by 5 more. The following year 12 Folland Gnats were ordered, including two equipped for fighter-reconnaissance duties, and in 1957 the wings were redesignated, being named after the provinces in which

Potez 25A–2, a French reconnaissance-bomber purchased for comparative trials with the Aero designs, but not ordered in quantity. (E. Ritaranta).

finally disappearing, while the others became:—

1 Lennosto, Luonetjarvi (ex LeR 4) with one flight of Bf 109G-6s and one flight of Bristol Blenheim Is and IVs for reconnaissance purposes.

2 Lennosto, Pori (ex LeR 1) HävLv 11 and 13, with Messerschmitt Bf 109G-6s being replaced by Valmet Vihuri Is as interim equipment, as these became available.

3 Lennosto, Utti (ex LeR 3) HävLv 31 and 33 with Messerschmitt Bf 109G-6s. This was for the time being, the main operational unit

During 1952 and 1953 30 Vihuris were built, and in the latter year 6 De Havilland Vampire F.B. 52s were purchased from Great Britain—the first new operational equipment for nine years, and the first jets to enter service with the Finnish Air Force; these were issued to

they were based, rather than numbered; thus, 1 Lennosto became the Häme Lennosto, 2 Lennosto became the Satakunta Lennosto and 3 Lennosto became the Karjala Lennosto.

Major re-equipment was now planned and in 1958 two new training types were ordered, the Saab 91D Safir from Sweden, and the Potez CM 170 Magister from France; a manufacturing licence for the latter type was also negotiated and 62 were to be built in Finland. On 1 August that year the flights of the Häme Lennosto were disbanded, the Blenheims, the last of the wartime aircraft still in service, finally being retired. At the same time HävLv 21 as re-activated to operate the Gnats, and HävLv 33 was disbanded, a transport and reconnaissance flight being formed in its stead, for which Douglas C-47s and Hunting-Percival Pembroke Mk.53s were acquired.

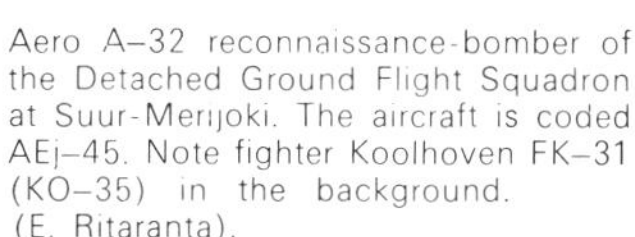

Aero A–32 reconnaissance-bomber of the Detached Ground Flight Squadron at Suur-Merijoki. The aircraft is coded AEj–45. Note fighter Koolhoven FK–31 (KO–35) in the background. (E. Ritaranta).

D.H. 60X Moth trainer licence-produced during the thirties. This aircraft is seen at Siikakangas in June 1941. (B. Hielm).

In 1961 HävLv 13 was disbanded, and the Vampire-equipped HävLv 11 and Gnat-equipped HävLv 21 exchanged numbers. Next year a full transport squadron was formed from the existing flight, this being responsible for aerial photo-survey and target-towing duties, and for the latter 4 Ilyushin Il-28 jet bombers were acquired from Russia. This country now became Finland's main supplier of aircraft, and a number of Mi 1 and Mi 4 helicopters were also obtained.

Plans for an advanced air defence network neared fruition in 1962 when 19 MiG-21F fighters and 2 MiG-21UTI conversion trainers were ordered, a high-powered radar network also being installed. An adjustment to the Peace Treaty was necessary for the acquisition of this equipment to allow for the air-to-air missiles carried by the MiGs. Deliveries began in April 1963, and by early 1965 all had been delivered to HävLv 31, and as it was the direct descendant of the wartime HLeLv 24, all aircraft were soon marked with that unit's Lynx insignia. Four MiG-15UTIs were also supplied for more elementary conversion training from such aircraft as the Vampire, and these also went to the same squadron. By 1965 the Vampires had all gone, and in 1967 more MiG-21Fs were ordered for the partial re-equipment of HävLv 11, the Gnats being relegated to the fighter/trainer role, though retaining their operational capability.

The present day air force is planned to have a strength of three squadrons of MiG-21Fs, one in each of the three wings, and has its headquarters in Helsinki. The Häme Lennosto, which incorporates HävLv 11, is at Jyväskylä, Luonetjarvi, the Karjala Lennosto, incorporating HävLv 31, at Kuopio, Rissala, and the Satakunta Lennosto, incorporating HävLv 21, at Pori. The Transport squadron is based at Utti, with one flight of fixed-wing aircraft and one of helicopters, the Depot is still at Tampere, the Aviation and Technical Schools are at Kauhava, while the Air Signals School is at Luonetjarvi with the Häme Lennosto. At Halli is the aircraft repair centre. Flying equipment is:—

Operational: MiG-21F, Folland Gnat.

Transport and target-towing: Douglas C-47, Hunting-Percival Pembroke 53, Ilyushin Il-28, Mi-4.

Advanced trainers: MiG-21UTI, MiG-15UTI, Potez CM 170 Magister.

Primary trainers and Communication aircraft: Saab 91D Safir, De Havilland (Canada) DHC-2 Beaver, Sud Alouette II, Augusta-Bell 206A Jet Ranger.

Camouflage and Markings

Until the late thirties no specific camouflage scheme was adopted for Finnish aircraft, many remaining in natural metal or silver-doped fabric finish, others carrying the paint scheme in which they were delivered. With the war clouds darkening, it became desirable to adopt a uniform pattern that would provide minimum visibility when aircraft were dispersed on the ground, or when seen from above while flying at low altitude. Starting with the Bristol Blenheim I, aircraft were to be painted olive green drab above, and very light grey underneath, and by the Winter War began in late 1939 all aircraft in operational service were painted in this manner. The national marking, a light blue swastika on a white circle, was carried in six positions, above and below the wings, and on the fuselage sides. On some types a very small reproduction of this marking was carried on the propellor blades. The aircraft serial was painted in black on the rear fuselage sides, between the national marking and

Licence-built Gloster Gamecock II (GA–52) of LLv 24 at Utti. (E. Ritaranta).

One of the original 7 Fokker D.XXIs purchased from Holland in 1937, FR-79 is seen here fitted with skis during its first winter in Finland. At this stage these aircraft were silver-doped on the under surfaces. (E. Ritaranta).

the tail unit.

During the Winter War numerous aircraft arrived from abroad, and initially these were operated in the camouflage schemes in which they were delivered, only Finnish national markings and serials being painted on; Hurricanes, Gladiators, Blenheims, Gauntlets and Lysanders from the United Kingdom were camouflaged in the R.A.F. scheme of green and brown above, the undersides being divided down the centre line of the fighters and reconnaissance types, port being black and starboard white, while the bombers were all-black below. French Morane 406s and Caudron C.714s were in typical French Armee de l'Air camouflage, Fiat G-50s carried the Italian home-based units' scheme, and Brewster 239s from America were overall pale grey in most cases, though a few were natural metal.

In the period between the wars, in the Spring of 1941, a new scheme was introduced featuring black and forest green camouflage patches on the upper surfaces and pale blue below. The serials were painted black on green or blue background, but where they ran across segments of black paint, were in green, in some cases a letter or a number being partly green and partly black. All aircraft already camouflaged in other schemes were repainted in this way when wear and tear dictated that this should take place, or when major servicing or other such opportunities occurred, while others such as the Brewster 239s were finished in the new scheme at once. After the start of the Continuation War all aircraft were painted with standard Axis recognition markings, comprising a metre-wide yellow band round the rear fuselage, and yellow undersides to the wingtips. Shortly after this, single-engined aircraft also featured a yellow band around the nose cowling.

During the Winter War a few aircraft had been painted all-white on the upper surface as snow camouflage, and during the Continuation War some aircraft, noteably the Brewster 239s, had patches of white distemper daubed in a rather haphazard manner, mainly over the black portions of their camouflage during the periods of snow. It should be noted that during the winters some Finnish aircraft, particularly the Fokker D.XXIs and Bristol Blenheim Is, were sometimes fitted with skis for operations, but although other types, including the Morane 406 and Brewster 239 were experimentally fitted with these, they were not used operationally by them. Right from the start, fighter pilots indicated their individual victories on the fins or rudders of their aiircraft. Fokker D.XXIs during the Winter War featured small white stripes on the rudders, very similar to the victory bars used on German fighters, and early in the Continuation War various methods of denoting score were used; the G-50 pilots of HLeLv 26 continued to use stripes, but differentiated in colour between aircraft claimed in the earlier conflict and this one; Oiva Tuominen also used a horizontal bar to indicate an aircraft destroyed on the ground. Several Brewster pilots painted a small frontal silhouette of the type claimed, but as scores rose this method became impracticable as it took up too much space. In 1942 Capt. Luukkanen of this squadron, HLeLv 24, was indicating his score by sticking the labels from beer bottles on the fin of his aircraft. Later in the war, most pilots reverted to the simple stripe.

The first German aircraft to be received from the Luftwaffe, the Dornier Do 17Z-2s, were soon painted in the black and green scheme, but later acquisitions such as the Junkers Ju 88A-4 and Messerschmitt Bf 109G-2 and 6s retained their German camouflage until they required repainting, which in many cases was not until after the Armistice. The Bf 109G-6s which equipped the air force postwar were finished in the black/green scheme, but on new acquisitions after the war this was abandoned, Vilhuris and Vampires being left natural metal, while Folland Gnats were delivered in R.A.F. Fighter Command green and grey with silver undersides. Mi-1 and Mi-4 helicopters from Russia were painted olive drab, but Il-28s, MiG-23Fs and -23UTIs, and MiG-15UTIs were all left natural metal.

Immediately following the Armistice in September 1944, the national marking was changed; by this time the swastika had gained a notorious reputation totally unrelated to the Finnish use of this symbol, and consequently a small white/light blue/white roundel was substituted to avoid any confusion should Finnish aircraft meet Soviet aircraft in the air. Several units carried special markings illustrated within this volume, the most famous of which was the black Lynx of HLeLv 24/HävLv 31.

The first Fokker D.XXI to be delivered to the Finns, FR-76, seen here in pristine finish before delivery to HLeLv 24 at Utti.   (G. Kamphuis).

Fokker D.XXI (FR–116) of HLeLv 24 during the Winter War. FR–114 and a third aircraft are in the background. (E. Ritaranta via C. F. Shores).

Another view of FR–116. At this time these aircraft were painted olive drab green above and pale grey below. Codes were in black. (E. Ritaranta via C. F. Shores).

Above: Fokker D.XXI of HLeLv 24 on skis during the winter of 1939/40.

Below: Fokker C.VE of TLeLv 14 on skis during the Winter War.   (B. Hielm).

Above: Fokker C.VE (FO–65) in factory-fresh paintwork, immediately after delivery. Note that this aircraft still retains the Townsend ring cowling at this stage. (G. Kamphuis).

Right: Another photograph of FO–65 shortly after delivery. (E. Ritaranta).

Left: Fokker C.X reconnaissance-bomber, a very successful type during the Winter War. This is FK–78, one of the Fokker-built aircraft purchased in 1937. (J. Alexander via C. F Shores).

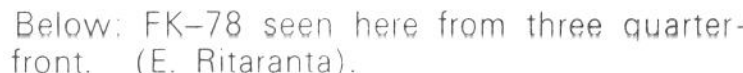

Below: FK–78 seen here from three quarter-front. (E. Ritaranta).

Above: One of the first Bristol Blenheim Is to be delivered from England, BL–104 is here seen fitted with skis shortly after arrival. (J. Alexander via C. F. Shores).

Above: Bristol Blenheim IV BL–124 purchased from the United Kingdom, ex-R.A.F. in early 1940 and issued to PLeLv 44. (B. Hielm).

Above & below: Two photographs of BL–139, one of the licence-built Blenheim Is, seen here at Siikakangas in June 1941. (B. Hielm).

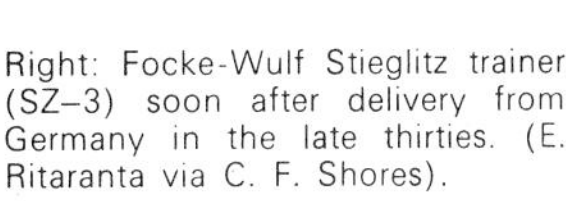

Right: Focke-Wulf Stieglitz trainer (SZ–3) soon after delivery from Germany in the late thirties. (E. Ritaranta via C. F. Shores).

Below: Morane-Saulnier M.S.50 trainer (coded 2C6, one of 6 such aircraft purchased. (E. Ritaranta).

V.L. Tuisku trainer (TU–171) at Siikakangas, June 1941. (B. Hielm).

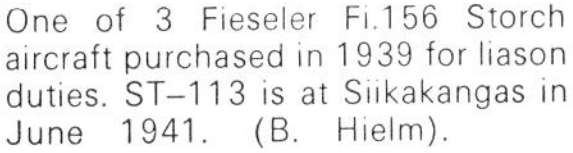

One of 3 Fieseler Fi.156 Storch aircraft purchased in 1939 for liason duties. ST–113 is at Siikakangas in June 1941. (B. Hielm).

Left: Gloster Gamecock II used during the Winter War for fighter training after being replaced in HLeLv 24 by Fokker D.XXIs. GA–51 is seen here fitted with skis for winter operations at Kauhava. (E. Ritaranta).

Below: Also used for fighter training after replacement by Gloster Gladiators in HLeLv 26, was this ski-equipped Bristol Bulldog IVA. (E. Ritaranta via C. F. Shores).

Left: Bristol Bulldog IVA while still in service as a fighter with HLeLv 26. (E. Ritaranta).

Below: Presented to the Finns by the sympathetic Swedes in 1940, and converted for use as a night bomber, Douglas DC–2, known in Finland as "Hanssin Jukka" and coded DC–1. (B. Hielm).

Above: Avro Anson I crew trainer, one of three serving with PLeLv 46 at Luonetjarvi in 1939. (E. Ritaranta via C. F. Shores).

Above: Received from England as a gift in February 1940, here is Gloster Gauntlet II GT-408 one of 24 delivered, fitted with skis and used as a fighter-trainer. (E. Ritaranta via C. F. Shores).

Left: One of the first Fiat G-50s to be delivered in early 1940. This aircraft, FA-17, is painted in the Finnish scheme of olive drab and grey. Note that on this aircraft the code is carried beneath the wing just inboard of the national marking. (E. Ritaranta via C. F. Shores).

Below: Fiat G-50 issued to HLeLv 26 in March 1940 to replace that unit's Gladiator IIs. Note Italian Regia Aeronautica home-based aircraft camouflage. This aircraft is FA-33. (E. Ritaranta)

Left: Brewster 239 fitted experimentally with skis during the period between the wars. Note this aircraft is painted in U.S. Navy pale grey. (E. Ritaranta).

Right: One of the first Brewster 239s to be delivered, issued in early 1940 to HLeLv 22, the foreign volunteer unit which was just forming. Note that this aircraft is natural metal finish. (E. Ritaranta).

Below: Polikarpov I–15bis fighter captured from the Russians during the Winter War, repaired by the State Aircraft Factory, and used as a trainer. Coded VH–11. (M. Salo).

Below: Polikarpov I–153 fighter captured during the Winter War, seen here fitted with skis. This aircraft was later pressed into front line service in TLeLv 30. Coded IT–101. (E. Ritaranta).

Above: A pair of Hawker Hurricane Is in service with HLeLv 30 during the period between the wars. These aircraft still retain their R.A.F. camouflage, the nearest aircraft being coded HC–458, and that in the background, HC–457. (E. Ritaranta via C. F. Shores).

Left: Captured Polikarpov I–16 fighter fitted with skis and used for training and evaluation. Coded VH–201. (E. Ritaranta).

Curtiss Hawk 75A–6, ex-Norwegian, sold to the Finns by Germany and seen here after issue to TLeLv 14 just before the start of the Continuation War. The aircraft is coded CU–564. Note Smolik trainer, SM–130 in background. (E. Ritaranta via C. F. Shores).

Curtiss Hawk 75A early in the Continuation War, before repainting in the black and green Finnish camouflage. Note yellow bands on cowling and beneath wingtips, but no band on fuselage. This aircraft, CU–551, is believed to be in service with TLeLv 14, just before being handed to HLeLv 32. (E. Ritaranta).

Above: The first V.L.-built Fokker D.XXI with Pratt and Whitney Twin Wasp Jr. engine and all-wing mounted armament. This aircraft has been finished in the black and green camouflage scheme, but carries no yellow identification markings, indicating that this photograph was taken before the start of the Continuation War. The aircraft is FR–150. (G. Kamphuis).

Left: Fokker D.XXI (Twin Wasp Jr.) of one of the reconnaissance units during the Continuation War. FR–143 is possibly an aircraft of TLeLv 16. Note yellow cowl and fuselage bands, and white markings on rudder. (E. Ritaranta via C. F. Shores).

Right: Another view of FR–150. This aircraft features an experimental extended glazing to the rear of the cockpit canopy. (G. Kamphuis).

Below: A pair of Fokker D.XXI (Twin Wasp Jr.) fighters of HLeLv 30 just before the start of the Continuation War. Nearest aircraft is FR–140. (G. Kamphuis).

Right: Fokker D.XXI (Twin Wasp Jr.) of unknown unit during the Continuation War. Note specially camouflaged wheel spats. Aircraft is FR–125. (C–J. Ehrengardt via C. F. Shores).

Left: Two more D.XXI (Twin Wasp Jr.) aircraft of unknown unit. Nearest aircraft is FR–124. (G. Kamphuis).

Left: D.XXI (Twin Wasp Jr.) FR–129 with extended cockpit canopy glazing and skis. (B. Hielm).

Below: D.XXI (Twin Wasp Jr.) FR–107, experimentally fitted with a retractable undercarriage. The small improvement in performance did not warrant production of the type. (G. Kamphuis).

Left: Brewster 239 of HLeLv 24 during the Continuation War. Note 'Lynx' unit insignia and personal marking on fin of BW–387 (E. Ritaranta via C. F. Shores).

Right: Another HLeLv 24 Brewster 239, this time BW–372. (E. Ritaranta).

Below: BW–372 seen from the front three-quarter view.

Right: Sgt. Erik Lyley (17½ victories) of HLeLv 24 with his Brewster, showing the personal insignia carried on the fin. This picture was taken at Kilpasilta in 1943. (B. Hielm).

Below: Lt. Lauri Nissinen of HLeLv 24, who gained many of his 32½ victories on Brewsters, seen here at Suulajarvi in 1942. The fin of his aircraft shows how many of the pilots of this unit identified their victories by frontal silhouettes of the type shot down during the earlier years of the Continuation War. (B. Hielm).

A pilot of HLeLv 24 climbs into the cockpit of Brewster 239 BW–364. (via C. F. Shores).

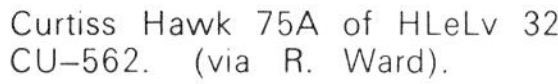

Curtiss Hawk 75A of HLeLv 32 CU–562. (via R. Ward).

Curtiss Hawk 75A of HLeLv 32. This aircraft is CU–553. (E. Ritaranta via C. F. Shores).

Curtiss Hawk 75A CU–562 of HLeLv 32 with ground crew of this squadron. (E. Ritaranta via C. F. Shores).

Fiat G–50, FA–17, one of, if not the, first of these aircraft to be delivered to Finland, seen here in service with HLeLv 26 during the Continuation War. Note that the original Italian camouflage has been very thinly over-sprayed with olive drab, and that the original Italian serial is still marked on the rear fuselage (3599). (via R. Ward).

FA–22 of HLeLv 26 in black/green camouflage. This is the aircraft of Pilot Lt. Joroinen. Note that FA–17, still finished olive drab, is in the background. This picture was taken in June 1941. (B. Hielm).

Line of HLeLv 26 G–50s at Vitele in September 1941. The aircraft in the foreground in original Italian camouflage is FA–26, Italian serial 4743, the aircraft flown by Flt. Mstr. Oiva Tuominen. (See colour illustration). (B. Hielm).

Right: Another shot of Joroinen's FA–22 while still in Italian camouflage. (B. Hielm).

Below: G–50 in black/green camouflage. (B. Hielm)

Below: G–50 FA–19 in black/green camouflage later in the Continuation War. Note white markings on rudder. (E. Ritaranta).

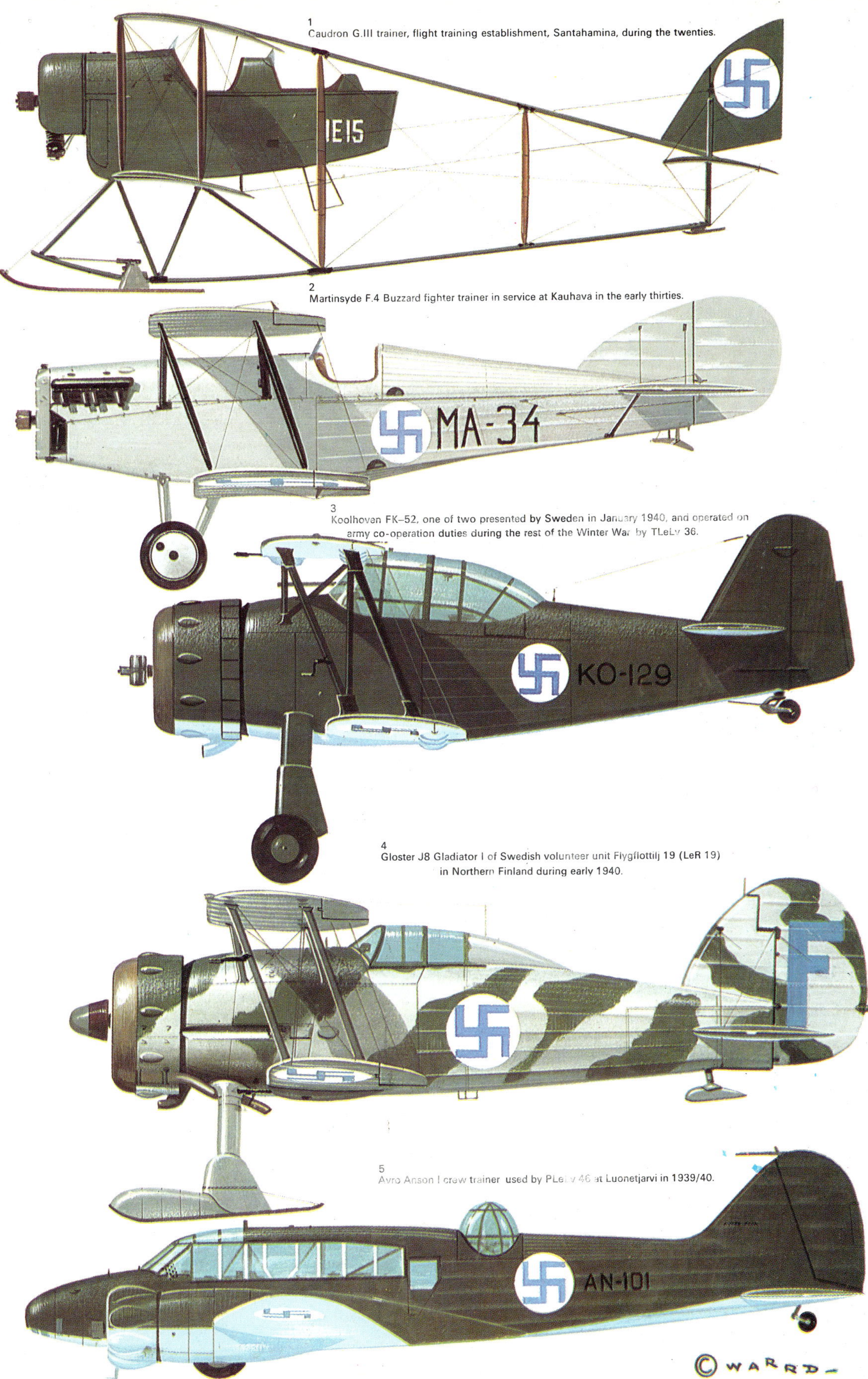

1 Caudron G.III trainer, flight training establishment, Santahamina, during the twenties.

2 Martinsyde F.4 Buzzard fighter trainer in service at Kauhava in the early thirties.

3 Koolhoven FK–52, one of two presented by Sweden in January 1940, and operated on army co-operation duties during the rest of the Winter War by TLeLv 36.

4 Gloster J8 Gladiator I of Swedish volunteer unit Flygflottilj 19 (LeR 19) in Northern Finland during early 1940.

5 Avro Anson I crew trainer used by PLeLv 46 at Luonetjarvi in 1939/40.

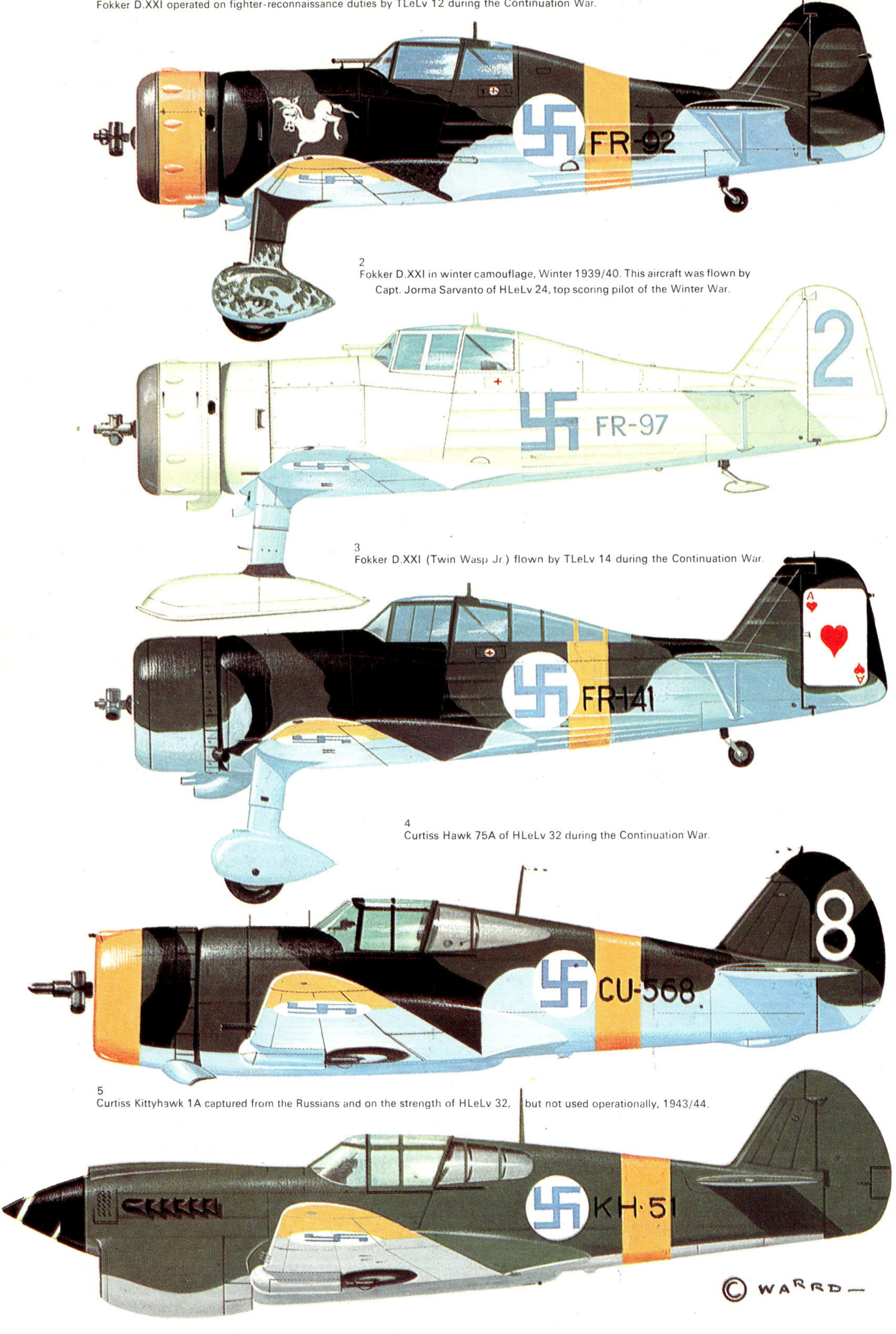

1
Fokker D.XXI operated on fighter-reconnaissance duties by TLeLv 12 during the Continuation War.

2
Fokker D.XXI in winter camouflage, Winter 1939/40. This aircraft was flown by Capt. Jorma Sarvanto of HLeLv 24, top scoring pilot of the Winter War.

3
Fokker D.XXI (Twin Wasp Jr.) flown by TLeLv 14 during the Continuation War.

4
Curtiss Hawk 75A of HLeLv 32 during the Continuation War.

5
Curtiss Kittyhawk 1A captured from the Russians and on the strength of HLeLv 32, but not used operationally, 1943/44.

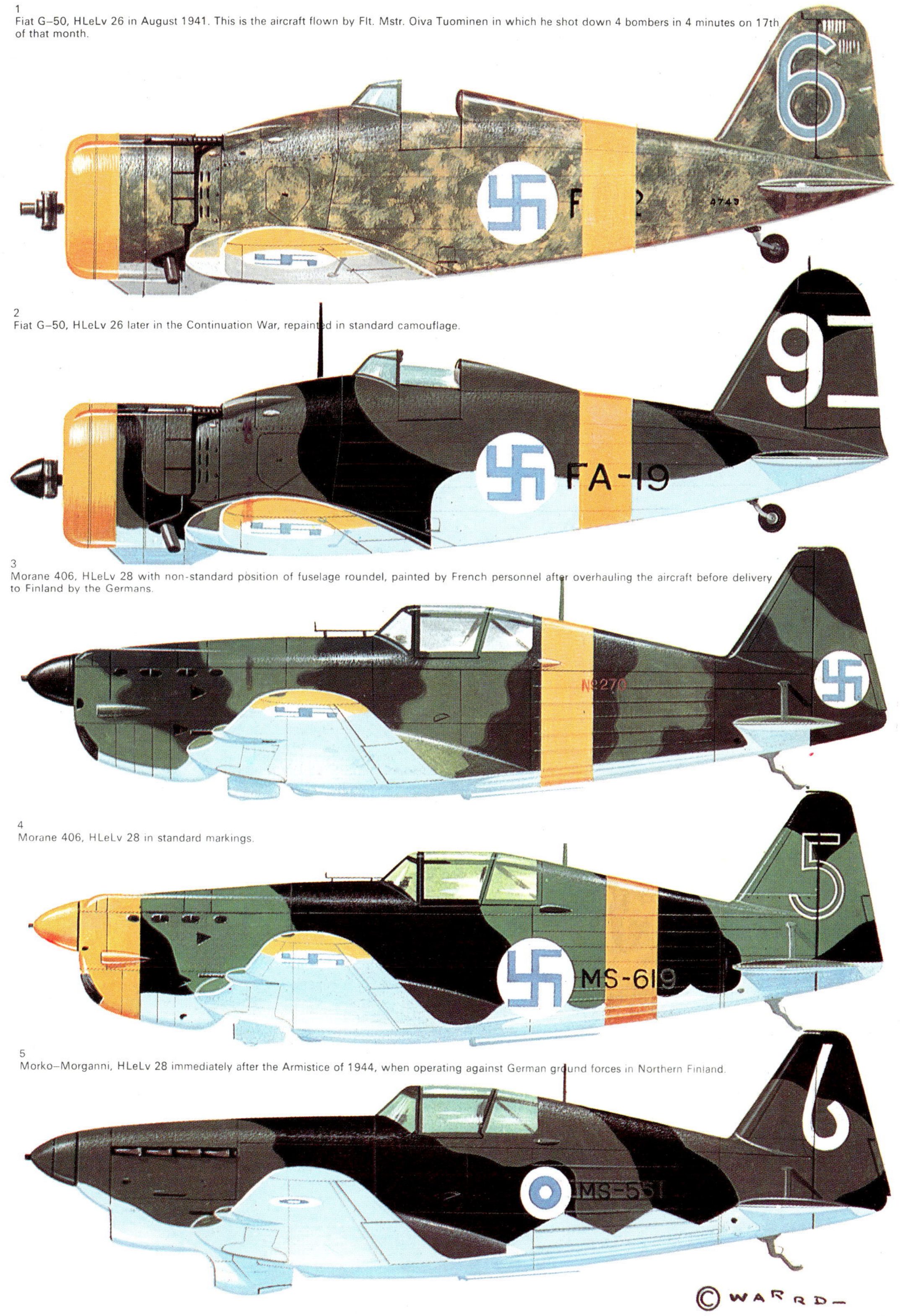

1
Fiat G–50, HLeLv 26 in August 1941. This is the aircraft flown by Flt. Mstr. Oiva Tuominen in which he shot down 4 bombers in 4 minutes on 17th of that month.

2
Fiat G–50, HLeLv 26 later in the Continuation War, repainted in standard camouflage.

3
Morane 406, HLeLv 28 with non-standard position of fuselage roundel, painted by French personnel after overhauling the aircraft before delivery to Finland by the Germans.

4
Morane 406, HLeLv 28 in standard markings.

5
Morko–Morganni, HLeLv 28 immediately after the Armistice of 1944, when operating against German ground forces in Northern Finland.

D

1
Bristol Blenheim I delivered from the United Kingdom in February 1940 (ex R.A.F.) and used to form PLeLv 42

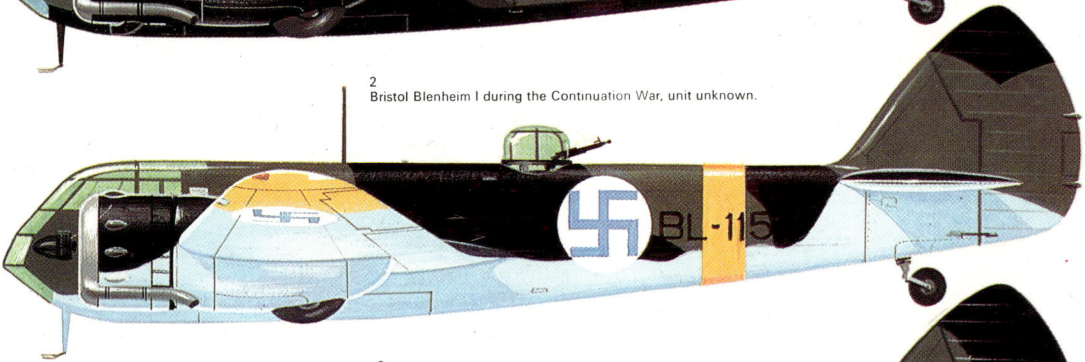

2
Bristol Blenheim I during the Continuation War, unit unknown.

3
Bristol Blenheim IV, PLeLv 46 early in the Continuation War.

4
Bristol Blenheim IV, PLeLv 46 in June 1941.

5
Junkers Ju 88A–4, PLeLv 44 in 1943.

6
Junkers Ju 88A–4, PLeLv 43 at Luonetjarvi in 1945.

© WARD

1
Dornier Do 17Z–2, PLeLv 46 in 1942, while still in Luftwaffe camouflage.
DN–79
2
Dornier Do 17Z–2, PLeLv 46 in 1943, after repainting in standard camouflage.
DN–60
3
Dornier Do 17Z–2 used in 1943 by a special long-range photo-reconnaissance flight. Note Ace of Spades insignia on nose, and winter camouflage.
DN–64
4
Tupolev SB–2bis, TLeLv 6 in early 1941 just before the start of the Continuation War.
5
Ilyushin DB–3 bomber, unit unknown, early in 1941.
6
Petlyakov Pe–2 of the long-range reconnaissance flight of PLeLv 48.
PE–211
© WARD

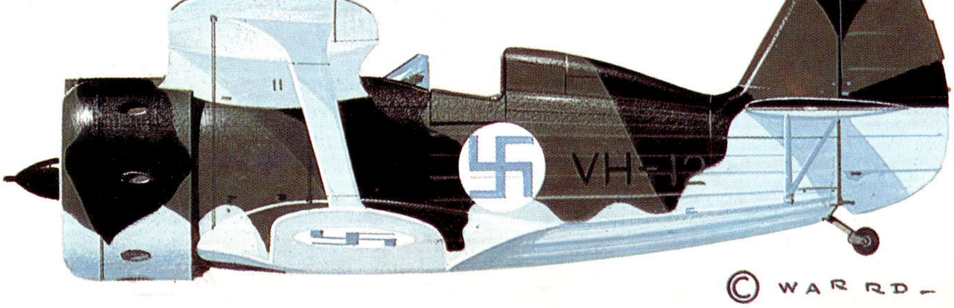

7
TLeLv 14.

8
HLeLv 24, and later of HavLv 31.

9
HLeLv 24, 2nd Flight.

10
PLeLv 46, later HavLv 11.

11
PLeLv 48.

12
HLeLv/HavLv 13 4.12.44–1.9.61,
and of HavLv 21 from 1.5.62.

1
Brewster 239, HLeLv 24's 1st Flight at Mikkeli, 1941. Pilot Lt. Olli Mustonen.

2
Brewster 239, HLeLv 24 in full Continuation War markings. Pilot Capt. Eino Luukkanen (54 victories).

3
Brewster 239, HLeLv 24 in winter camouflage.

4
Brewster 239, HLeLv 24's 2nd Flight at Tiiksjarvi, 1942. Ensign Heimo Lampi (14 victories).

5
Brewster 239, HLeLv 24 in winter camouflage, 1942. Pilot Flt. Mstr. Nils Katajainen (36 victories).

6
Polikarpov I–153 after overhaul by the State Aircraft Factory. This aircraft was later used by TLeLv 30,
recorded in the IT range and carrying yellow identification bands.

© WAR RD

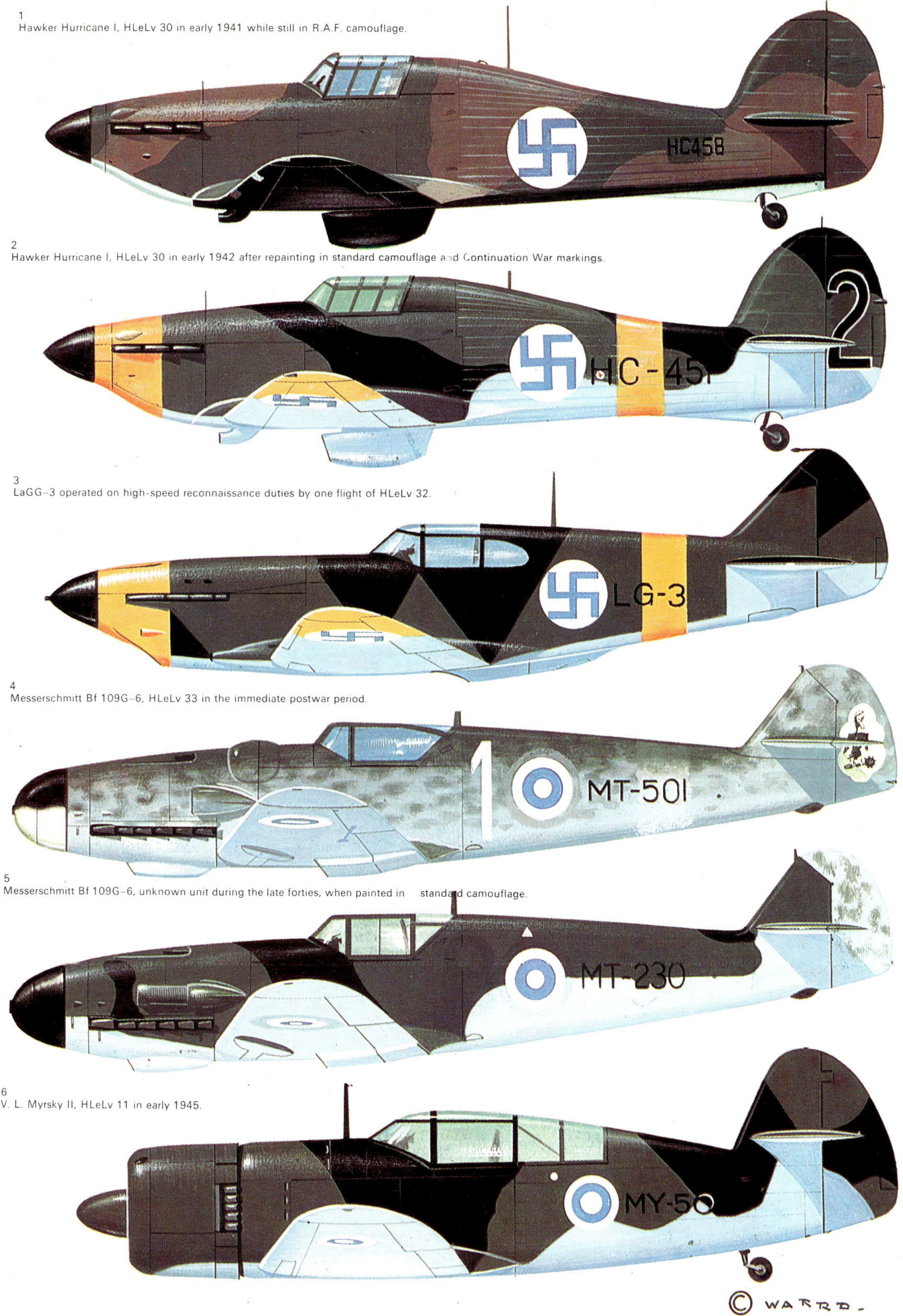

1
Hawker Hurricane I, HLeLv 30 in early 1941 while still in R.A.F. camouflage.

2
Hawker Hurricane I, HLeLv 30 in early 1942 after repainting in standard camouflage and Continuation War markings.

3
LaGG-3 operated on high-speed reconnaissance duties by one flight of HLeLv 32.

4
Messerschmitt Bf 109G-6, HLeLv 33 in the immediate postwar period.

5
Messerschmitt Bf 109G-6, unknown unit during the late forties, when painted in standard camouflage.

6
V. L. Myrsky II, HLeLv 11 in early 1945.

1
Valmet Vihuri, HavLv 33 in the mid fifties.

2
Saab 91D Safir, Kauhava training school.

3
Folland Gnat, HavLv 21 in the late fifties.

4
MiG 21F, HavLv 31, Karjala Lennosto, Rissala, 1969.

5
De Havilland Vampire F.B.52, HavLv 11, late fifties.

6
Ilyushin Il–28 target-towing aircraft of the Transport Squadron at Utti, 1967.

Above: G-50 FA-22 after re-painting in black/green camouflage, with rudder number changed from '3' to '4'.

Left: Morane 406 of HLeLv 28. (B. Hielm via C-J. Ehrengardt).

Above: Morane 406 MS-619, of HLeLv 28 in typical markings. (E. Ritaranta via C. F. Shores).

Left: Morane 406 still in French camouflage when first issued to HLeLv 28 early in 1940. This aircraft is MS-318. (B. Hielm).

Below: Morane 406 MS-610 of HLeLv 28 undergoing engine service. (E. Ritaranta).

Above: Morane 406 MS–620 at dispersal in the Petroskoi area of Eastern Karelia.   (E. Ritaranta).

Above: A Morane 410 with four wing-mounted machine-guns instead of the usual two. This aircraft was one of the final batch of Moranes supplied to Finland in 19—. (G. Botquin via C–J. Ehrengardt).

Left: Gloster Gladiator II GL–274, operated as a tactical-reconnaissance fighter with TLeLv 16 throughout the Continuation War, seen here fitted with skis. (E. Ritaranta).

Below: Gladiator II GL–270 of TLeLv 16 at dispersal. Note that the white of the upper wing roundel has been painted out in favour of green to leave only a thin outline to the black swastika. This was done to assist the camouflage of these aircraft when operating at low level. (E. Ritaranta via C. F. Shores).

Right: Hawker Hurricane I of HLeLv 30 in Continuation War markings. This aircraft is HC–460. (E. Ritaranta via C. F. Shores).

Below: Hurricane I of HLeLv 30 running up its engine. (E. Ritaranta via C. F. Shores).

Below: LaGG–3, coded LG–3, one of 3 of these aircraft captured by the Germans, sold to the Finns, and operated by HLeLv 32 as a high-speed reconnaissance flight. (E. Ritaranta via C. F. Shores).

Below: V.L.Myrsky II, MY–5, an early production aircraft, issued to TLeLv 12 in August 1944. (via R. Ward).

Below: Polikarpov I–153, coded at this stage VH–12 (later coded in the IT range) in black/green camouflage. 21 of these aircraft were issued to TLeLv 30 for fighter-reconnaissance duties. (M. Salo).

Messerschmitt Bf 109G-2 of HLeLv 34 in 1943. Nearest aircraft is MT-229 and that in the background MT-218. (via R. Ward).

Bf 109G-2 MT-216 of HLeLv 34. (E. Ritaranta).

Bf. 109G-2 MT-210 of HLeLv 34, seen here at Malmi. (E. Ritaranta via C. Shores).

Right: Bf 109G-2 in dispersal, believed to be an aircraft of HLeLv 34. (E. Ritaranta).

Below: Bf 109G-2 MT-201, the first aircraft of the series, flown by Maj. Eino Luukkanen, commanding officer of HLeLv 34 in May 1943. (E. Ritaranta).

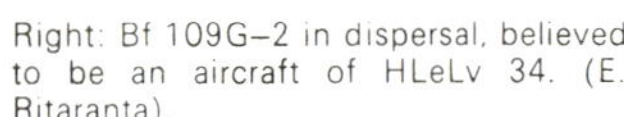

Above, left: Bristol Blenheim I BL–140, of PLeLv 48, nosed over at Ontolla, summer 1944. (B. Hielm).

Above, right: Plan view of Bristol Blenheim I, showing clearly the pattern of the black and green camouflage. (B. Hielm).

Left: Blenheim I fitted with retractable ski undercarriage for winter operations from Luonetjarvi in 1942. (B. Hielm).

Above: Blenheim I BL–115. This aircraft is carrying a German 7.7mm. MG 34 machine gun in the dorsal turret in place of the normal Lewis gun. (E. Ritaranta via C. F. Shores).

Below: Bristol Blenheim IV, BL–129, of PLeLv 46.   (E. Ritaranta via C. F. Shores).

Above: Dornier Do 17Z–2 of PLeLv 46 in 1943.   (E. Ritaranta via C. F. Shores).

Above, left: Nose of Do 17Z–2 of PLeLv 46, showing gun positions. (B. Hielm).

Above, right: Buffalo emblem of PLeLv 46 painted beneath the cockpit of a Do 17Z–2.   (B. Hielm).

Left: Air and ground crew of a Ju 88A–4 of PLeLv 44 prior to take off on a mission. (E. Ritaranta via C. F. Shores).

Below: Junkers Ju 88A–4 of PLeLv 44, JK–267, running up prior to take-off.   (via R. Ward).

Top & inset: Tupolev SB–2bis bomber, coded SB–11 and used by TLeLv 6 for sea reconnaissance and anti-submarine duties.   (E. Ritaranta via C. F. Shores).

Above: SB–2bis bombers of TLeLv 6 in flight over typical Finnish lakes. The nearest aircraft is SB–20.   (E. Ritaranta).

Right: SB–2bis come to grief following the collapse of the starboard under-carriage leg. Note diagonal stripe marking below port wing. (E. Ritaranta via C. F. Shores).

Below: Line of SBs of TLeLv 6. The first, second and fourth aircraft are SB–2bis models, the third is an SB–2. (W. B. Klepacki via C. F. Shores).

Left: Captured Beriev MBR–2 flying-boat, VV–18, one of 4 used by TLeLv 12, seen here on Lake Ladoga at Salmi in August 1941. (B. Hielm).

Below: Westland Lysander I of TLeLv 16 in 1941. The aircraft is coded LY–116. (E. Ritaranta via C. F. Shores).

Above: Fokker C.X operated by one of the reconnaissance squadrons. (E. Ritaranta via C. F. Shores).

Left: Fieseler Storch of the flying division devoted to liason and transportation duties, mounted on skis for snow operations. This is ST–112. (E. Ritaranta).

Right: Fieseler Storch ST–113 seen here during 1941, before the outbreak of the Continuation War. (B. Hielm).

Above: Heinkel He 115A-2, interned after escape from Norway in May 1940, and put into Finnish service. It is coded HE-115. (E. Ritaranta via C. F. Shores).

Above: Blackburn Ripon IIF, RI-151, of TLeLv 6 at the edge of a lake. (B. Hielm).

Left: Ripon IIF RI-151 in flight, showing to advantage the pattern of the upper surface camouflage.
(E. Ritaranta via C. F. Shores).

Below: Dornier Do 22K-1 of TLeLv 6. These aircraft were operated on skis, as seen here, and also on floats. This is DR-198. (E. Ritaranta via C. F. Shores).

Above: Gloster Gauntlet II fighter trainer at Kauhava in full Continuation War markings.   (E. Ritaranta)

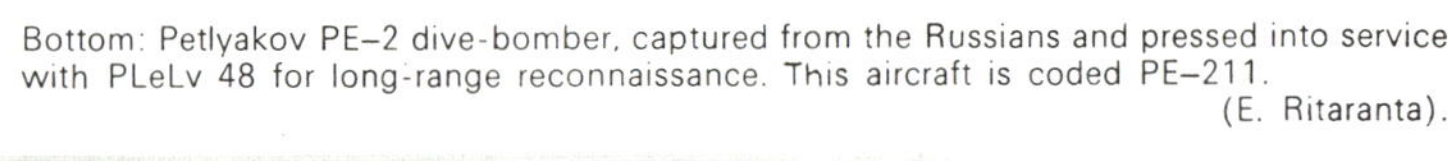

Above: Fokker C.VE of TLeLv 14, still in use during the Continuation War.   (E. Ritaranta via C. F. Shores).

Left: Another Gauntlet, GT–410, after coming to grief in a training accident. (E. Ritaranta via C. F. Shores).

Below: D.H. Moth primary trainer, MO–112, during the Continuation War.   (E. Ritaranta).

Bottom: Petlyakov PE–2 dive-bomber, captured from the Russians and pressed into service with PLeLv 48 for long-range reconnaissance. This aircraft is coded PE–211.
(E. Ritaranta).

Right: Ilyushin DB–3 bomber captured during the Winter War and put into service with one of the bomber squadrons. This aircraft was coded VP–101. (E. Ritaranta).

Above: DB–3, VP–14, at Siikakangas in June 1941.   (B. Hielm).

Above: A further view of VP–14 at Siikakangas. Note Blenheim I in background still in all-green finish.   (B. Hielm).

Dornier Do 17Z–2 with PLeLv 45 at Luonetjarvi after the war. This photograph was taken in Spring 1948, just before the aircraft were taken out of service. (B. Hielm).

DC–2 "Hanssin Jukka" in service during the Continuation War as a transport. (B. Hielm).

Above: The V.L.Pyry II trainer, produced in 1941. This is PY–3 in early 1941.   (E. Ritaranta via C. F. Shores).

Above, left: The most successful of the Fiat G–50 pilots, Flt.Mstr. Oiva Tuominen of HLeLv 26, by the tail of his aircraft at Salmi in August 1941 with one of his ground crew. Note 8 Winter War, 4½ Continuation War and 1 ground victory. See colour illustration.   (B. Hielm).

Above, right: Dorsal turret and gunner of a Blenheim I in 1942.   (B. Hielm).

A pair of Junkers K.43s in use as transports during the Continuation War. (via C. F. Shores).

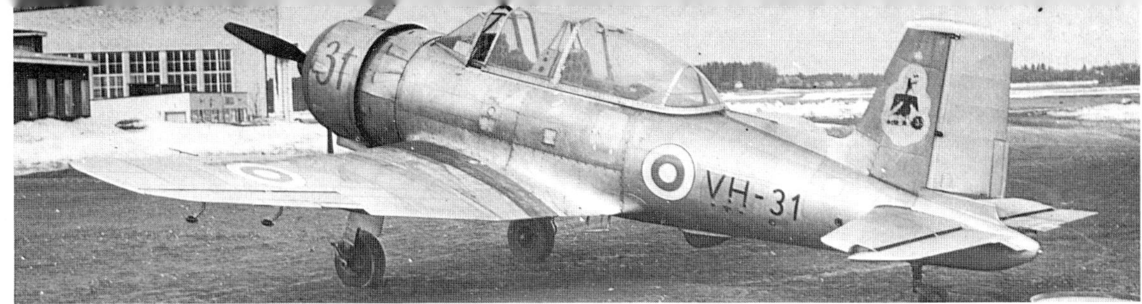

Above: Valmet Vihuri of HavLv 33 at Utti, part of 3 Lennosto.   (K. Niska).

Above: Valmet Vihuri of HavLv 31. Note 'Lynx' insignia beneath cockpit. Code is VH–44.   (K. Niska).
Below: D.H.Vampire F.B.52 of 2 Lennosto.   (K. Niska).

Below: D.H.Vampire T.55 jet conversion trainer of 2 Lennosto.   (K. Niska)

Below: Potez CM 170 Magister jet trainer of HavLv 21. Note duck insignia on nose.   (K. Niska).

Below: Saab 91D Safir trainer in flight.   (K. Niska).

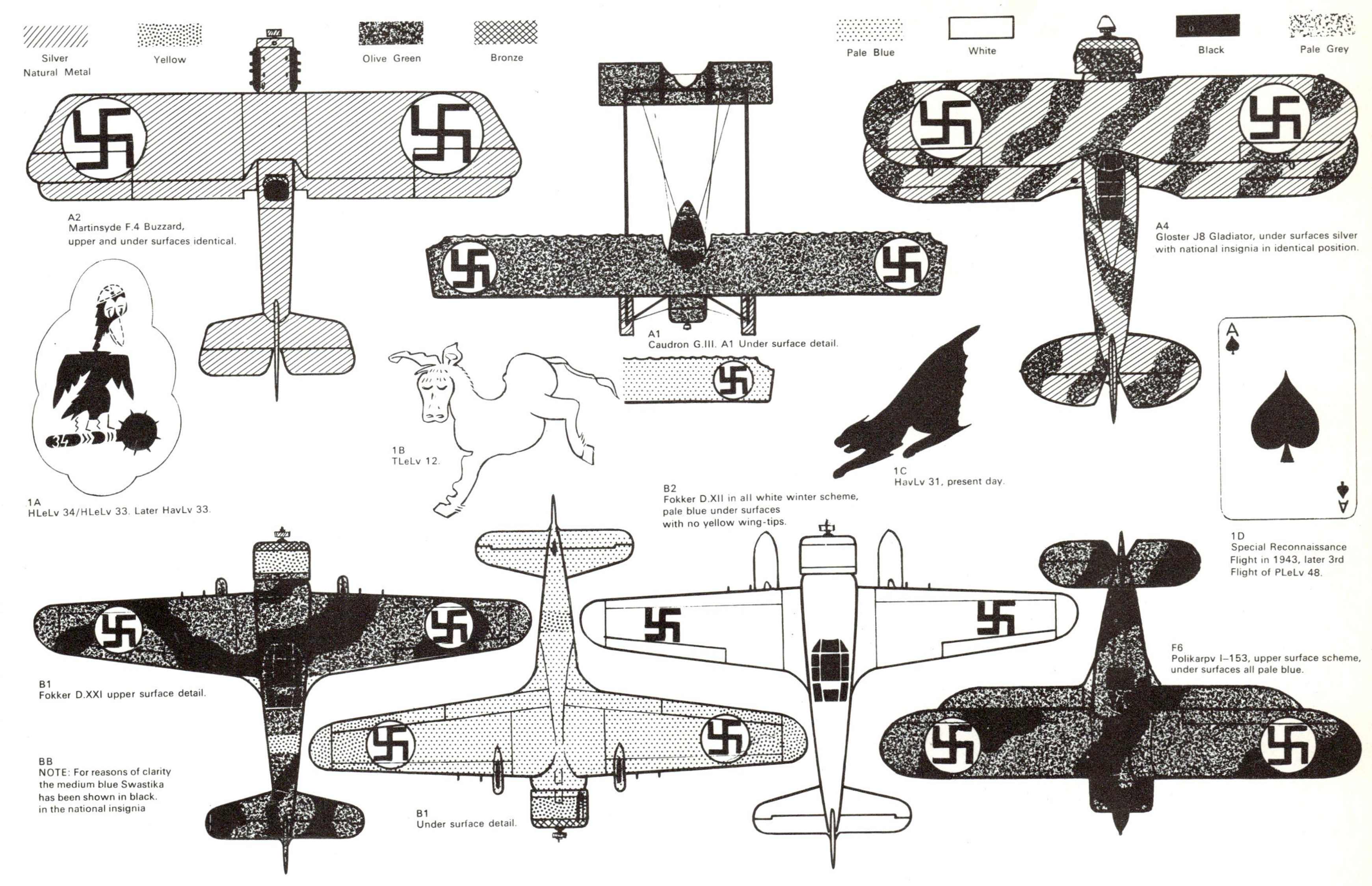

Silver Natural Metal
Yellow
Olive Green
Bronze
Pale Blue
White
Black
Pale Grey
A2
Martinsyde F.4 Buzzard, upper and under surfaces identical.
A1
Caudron G.III. A1 Under surface detail.
A4
Gloster J8 Gladiator, under surfaces silver with national insignia in identical position.
1A
HLeLv 34/HLeLv 33. Later HavLv 33.
1B
TLeLv 12.
B2
Fokker D.XII in all white winter scheme, pale blue under surfaces with no yellow wing-tips.
1C
HavLv 31, present day.
1D
Special Reconnaissance Flight in 1943, later 3rd Flight of PLeLv 48.
B1
Fokker D.XXI upper surface detail.
BB
NOTE: For reasons of clarity the medium blue Swastika has been shown in black. in the national insignia
B1
Under surface detail.
F6
Polikarpv I-153, upper surface scheme, under surfaces all pale blue.

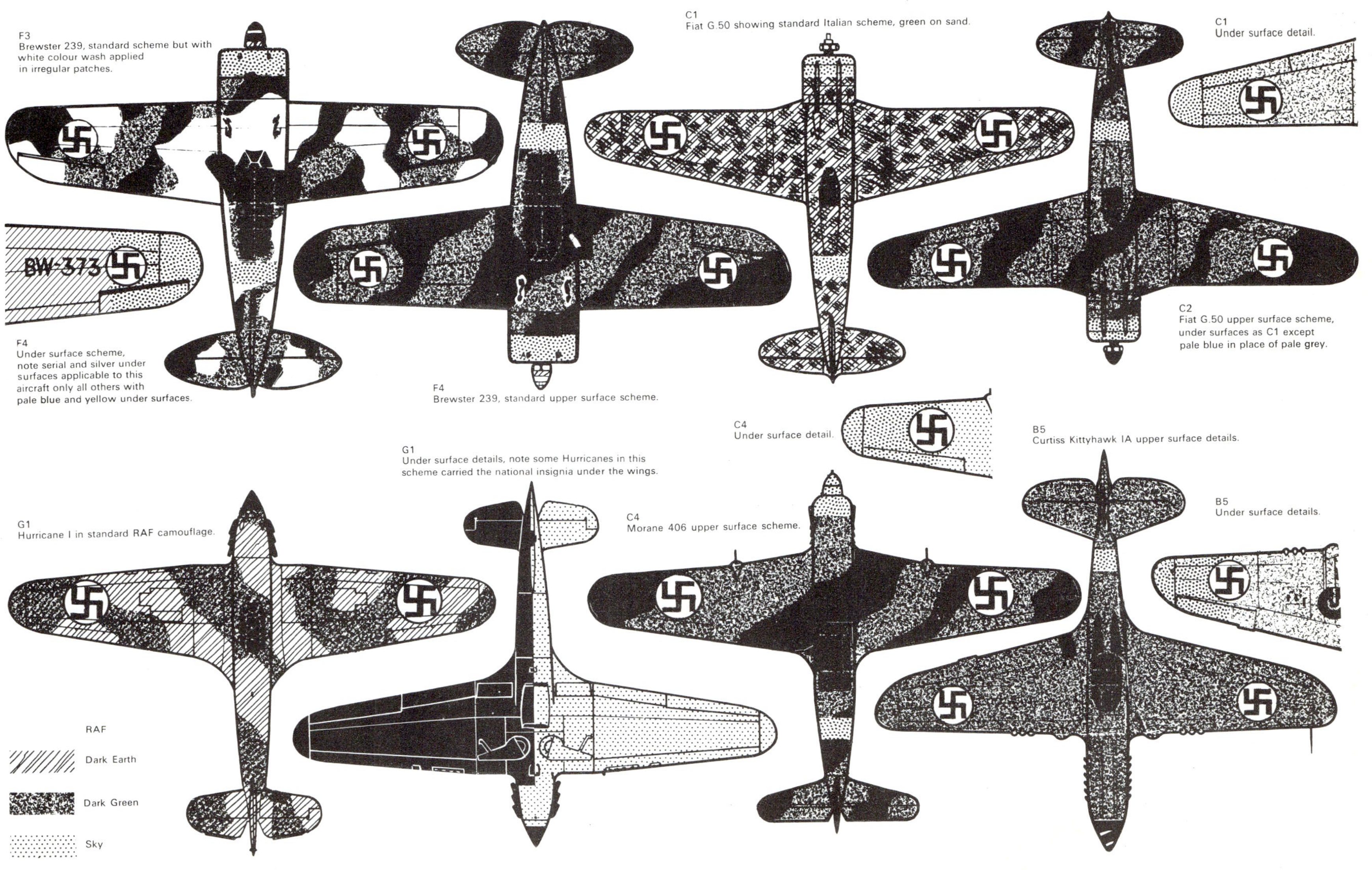

F3
Brewster 239, standard scheme but with white colour wash applied in irregular patches.

F4
Under surface scheme, note serial and silver under surfaces applicable to this aircraft only all others with pale blue and yellow under surfaces.

F4
Brewster 239, standard upper surface scheme.

C1
Fiat G.50 showing standard Italian scheme, green on sand.

C1
Under surface detail.

C2
Fiat G.50 upper surface scheme, under surfaces as C1 except pale blue in place of pale grey.

G1
Under surface details, note some Hurricanes in this scheme carried the national insignia under the wings.

G1
Hurricane I in standard RAF camouflage.

C4
Under surface detail.

C4
Morane 406 upper surface scheme.

B5
Curtiss Kittyhawk IA upper surface details.

B5
Under surface details.

G2
Hurricane I upper surface details.
G2
Under surface details.
E2
Dornier Do.17Z–2 upper surface scheme.
E3
Dornier Do.17Z–2 Winter scheme with black segments overpainted white.
B4
Under surface detail.
B4
Curtiss Hawk 75A upper surface scheme.
E2/3
Under surface detail.
D3
Under surface detail, applicable to Mk.I's also.
D4
Blenheim IV in overall olive green upper surfaces, June 1941.
H5
Vampire FB 52, upper and under surfaces identical.
G5
Messerschmitt Bf.109G in standard green/black camouflage, late forties. National insignia in same position on pale blue under surfaces.
D3
Blenheim IV standard upper surface camouflage scheme, Blenheim I's in very similar scheme.
D4
Under surface detail.